The Duchess
of Malfi

Crofts Classics

GENERAL EDITOR

Samuel H. Beer, *Harvard University*

JOHN WEBSTER

The Duchess
of Malfi

EDITED BY

Fred B. Millett

Harlan Davidson, Inc.
Arlington Heights, Illinois 60004

Library of Congress Cataloging-in-Publication Data

Webster, John, 1580?–1625?
    The Duchess of Malfi.

    (Crofts classics)
    Bibliography: p.
    1. Millett, Fred Benjamin, 1890–   . II. Title.
PR3184.D8   1985   822'.3   85-25283
ISBN 0-88295-101-7

Manufactured in the United States of America
93 92 91 90 20 21 22 CM

INTRODUCTION

Publication and Date. The title page of the first edition of *The Duchess of Malfi* (1623) bears the notation, "the perfect and exact copy, with diverse things printed that the length of the play would not bear in the presentment." It is doubtful whether the full text of Webster's tragedy has ever been acted on the public stage. The first quarto also contains a list of the actors' names. In some cases, two actors' names are assigned to a single role, and numbered 1 and 2. Thus, the role of Ferdinand was created by Richard Burbage, the greatest actor of the period and the creator of the title roles in Shakespeare's major tragedies, and was acted later by John Taylor. Since the role of Antonio was first acted by William Ostler, his death on December 16, 1614 furnishes one piece of evidence for the date of the play. As Webster is known to have been a slow writer, the tragedy was probably written in 1612-1613 and first acted in 1613-1614.

The play seems to have been revived in 1617. If Antonio's long speech in the first scene about affairs at the French court is actually a reference to the assassination of Marshall d'Ancre on April 14, 1617, the play must have been revised and revived in 1617, or shortly thereafter. The list of actors' names suggests a second revival at some time after the death of Burbage on March 13, 1619 and before the death of Nicholas Tooley in June, 1623. This revival may have been the occasion for the first printing of the play.

Source. The source of *The Duchess of Malfi* is, in all probability, William Painter's *The Palace of Pleasure* (1567). But this collection of tales was itself a translation of François de Belleforest's *Histoires Tragiques* (1565), and it in turn had been translated from Matteo Bandello's collection of *novelle,* the first of which were published in 1554. Since Bandello may have been an eye-witness of the murder of Antonio, Bandello himself may be represented by the character Delio in the play.

For the earlier part of the plot, up to the discovery of the identity of the Duchess' husband, Webster follows closely the action of Painter's tale, although he rejects the ambivalent attitude toward the Duchess— half reprobation of her immodesty and half sympathy for her widowed state. But Webster places the discovery of the Duchess' motherhood after the birth of the first and not the second child, and invents the manner of the discovery, Antonio's loss of the horoscope. He adds the accusation of Antonio as the peculator of the Duchess' wealth, and brings about the separation of the lovers before and not after their pursuers appear. He adds the sub-plot of Julia, and Castruccio becomes her husband, and not a Cardinal as he actually was. Bosola is transformed from the hired murderer of Antonio into one of the major figures in the play. The manner of the Duchess' tortures, of her brothers' deaths, and of Antonio's murder, that is, most of Acts IV and V, are Webster's additions to Painter's version of the story.

The Play. *The Duchess of Malfi* is a powerful example of the villain play, a type that developed out of the earlier revenge tragedy. One of the fundamental differences between the earlier type and Webster's play is the character of the villain. In *The Spanish Tragedy* and *Hamlet,* the avenger, the hero of the drama, was a sympathetic character who assumed, perhaps reluctantly, the moral responsibility of avenging the death of a close relative, a father or a son. In Webster's tragedy and others of the same decade, the situation is reversed. The avenger has now become the villain; the avenger's motives are evil and not good; the villain's victim is more or less innocent.

For the more overtly supernatural devices of the older type—the howling ghosts, the celestial portents

—Webster has substituted more naturalistic forms of premonition: the dreams, Antonio's nose-bleed and the dyeing of the initials in his handkerchief with blood, the tangling of the Duchess' hair, and the warning Echo. Webster also gives weighty emphasis, in the famous—or infamous—torture scenes, to the physical apparatus by means of which the victim is tormented. But Webster's most important contributions to the type are the constant foreshadowing of the tragic outcome —even in such light scenes as the wooing of Antonio and the badinage before the appearance of Ferdinand in the Duchess' bedchamber—and the emphasis on the malcontent's philosophizing on the essential human condition, the skull beneath the skin, the brevity and meaninglessness of life, the inescapable shadow that death casts over it, and the inordinate capacity of the human soul for evil and cruelty.

The plot of *The Duchess of Malfi* is not its strongest point. Its most obvious weakness is the inactivity of the brothers during the two years that pass between Act II and Act III. The brothers' delay in acting on the information they already have is inexplicable, and the reason for the lapse of time—the necessity of giving the Duchess as many children as the source of the story gave her—is dramatically irrelevant. The character of Julia is imperfectly integrated into the action of the play, and her sudden death—from kissing a poisoned book—is pure sensationalism. The device by which the Cardinal sets his own death-trap is preposterously out of character.

Despite the vivid and telling characterization, moreover, there is also an obvious weakness in this aspect of the play, the unsatisfactory motivation of the diabolical behavior of the brothers, especially of Ferdinand. It is not enough to say that this is a villain-play and that the Elizabethans were more than willing to take their villains on trust. One feels, particularly in the language and behavior of Duke Ferdinand, a violence disproportionate to the offense, even though we have been informed earlier of his potentially violent nature. One is tempted to find a motive for Ferdinand's violence not only in his unstable emotional temperament, affronted pride, and belatedly acknowledged greed but in an unconscious incestuous attachment to his sister. But Ferdinand is not altogether evil. The marriage of his beloved sister precipitates him into the intolerable anguish of sexual jealousy, but his very love of her arouses profound feelings of guilt. His only escape from the conflict between these violent and contradictory emotions is madness. Ferdinand's love of the Duchess destroys not only her but himself.

Aside from the lack of clarity in the motivation of Ferdinand, the characterization in *The Duchess of Malfi* is not only an important element in the effectiveness of the drama but one of the grounds for its great distinction. The Duchess and Bosola are remarkable character-creations for any stage for any time. The characterization of the Duchess gives us a superb portrait of a great Renaissance princess. In her exalted social position, she can afford to be unequivocably honest with herself, honest about her experiences, perfectly straightforward in her love of Antonio, her wooing of him, and her delight in their marital relations. Her honesty never fails her in the face of the agonies and the tortures she is forced to experience. The fact that her every speech rises from the very center of her being makes for an astounding effect of psychological reality and vitality. Her self-possession is never really shaken. Over and above her royal status, there are two major sources of her self-possession: her gradual acknowledgment that, to a degree, the suffering visited upon her by "Heaven's scourge-stick" is part and parcel of the scheme of things, and her unshaken conviction that there is an eternity beyond the mad evil world in which her brothers live and act. In the end, the Duchess' unshaken self-possession not only offers a needed counterpoise to the malignant evil with which she is surrounded but is the final source of the triumph of spirit that brings to the audience the needed tragic purgation of her and their emotions.

Bosola is a vastly more complex character than the

Duchess. He is, or, as Antonio suggests, at least pretends
to be a malcontent; his grim experience has led him to
an intense awareness of life's "wormy circumstance."
He makes a living as a villain's hireling, and serves his
master faithfully until he realizes that his master intends
to betray him and until he is moved by the nobility of
his victim. His encomium of Antonio after the Duchess'
apparent dismissal of him is certainly not utterly in-
sincere, and leads with complete plausibility to the
Duchess' confiding revelation of the identity of the
father of her children. Since he can no longer bear to be
seen by his victim in his own person, he hides his face
in a mask. The tears he sheds when he is left alone
after the death of the Duchess are real tears. There is
no doubt that for contemporary readers Bosola is the
most fascinating and intriguing character in the play.
It is not surprising, then, that Webster has given the
finest poetry in the play to this eternally ambiguous
figure, nor that the poetry is of so distinguished a quality
that it constitutes the major ground of the play's
greatness.

THE PRINCIPAL DATES
IN WEBSTER'S LIFE

1580   Conjectural date of Webster's birth.

1602   Collaborated with Munday, Middleton, Drayton, and others on a play entitled *Caesar's Fall;* with Dekker, Drayton, Middleton, and Munday on a play entitled *The Two Shapes* (?); with Dekker, Heywood, and Smith on a play entitled *Lady Jane Grey;* with Heywood on a play entitled *Christmas Comes But Once a Year.* These plays have not survived.

1602   Contributed prefatory verses to Munday's translation of *Palmerin of England.*

1603   Death of Queen Elizabeth; accession of James I.

1604   Contributed the induction to a revival of Marston's *The Malcontent.* Contributed a prefatory ode to Harrison's *Arches of Triumph.*

1607   *Westward Ho!* published as by Webster and Dekker. *Northward Ho!* published as by Webster and Dekker. *Sir Thomas Wyatt* published as by Webster and Dekker. (This play may contain portions of the earlier play *Lady Jane Grey.*

1612   Published *The White Devil.* Contributed prefatory verses to Heywood's *Apology for Actors.* Published *A Monumental Column,* an elegy on the death of Prince Henry.

1615   May have contributed additional "Characters" to the sixth edition of Sir Thomas Overbury's *Characters.*

1617   Was the object of satirical verses by Henry Fitzjeffrey in *Certain Elegies Done by Sundry Excellent Wits.*

1621   May have collaborated with Middleton on *Anything For a Quiet Life,* published in 1662.

1623   Published *The Duchess of Malfi.* Published *The Devil's Law-Case.*

1624   Composed *Monuments of Honour,* a Lord Mayor's Pageant for the Merchant-Taylors, of which he had been "born free." Collaborated with John Ford on a play, now lost, entitled *The Late Murder of the Son upon the Mother.*

1625   Death of James I; accession of Charles I. May have collaborated with Massinger and Ford on *The Fair Maid of the Inn,* published in 1647. May have collaborated with Rowley and Heywood on *A Cure for a Cuckold,* published in 1661.

Before 1634   Wrote, probably in collaboration, *Appius and Virginia,* published in 1654.

1634   Conjectural date of his death.

DRAMATIS PERSONAE

FERDINAND, Duke of Calabria
THE CARDINAL, his Brother
ANTONIO BOLOGNA, Steward of the household to the
    Duchess
DELIO, his Friend
DANIEL DE BOSOLA, Gentleman of the horse to the
    Duchess
CASTRUCCIO
MARQUIS OF PESCARA
COUNT MALATESTE
SILVIO, a Lord, of Milan ⎱ Gentlemen attending on
RODERIGO   ⎰   the Duchess
GRISOLAN
DOCTOR
Several Madmen, Pilgrims, Executioners, Officers, At-
    tendants, &c.

DUCHESS OF MALFI, sister of Ferdinand and the Cardinal
CARIOLA, her Woman
JULIA, Castruccio's Wife, and the Cardinal's Mistress
Old Lady, Ladies and Children

SCENE—*Amalfi, Rome, and Milan*

THE DUCHESS OF MALFI

Act I

SCENE I

(Enter ANTONIO *and* DELIO*)*

DELIO.   You are welcome to your country, dear An-
    tonio;
You have been long in France, and you return
A very formal Frenchman in your habit.
How do you like the French court?
    ANTONIO.   I admire it:
In seeking to reduce both state and people   5
To a fixed order, their judicious king
Begins at home; quits first his royal palace
Of flattering sycophants, of dissolute
And infamous persons, which he sweetly terms
His master's masterpiece, the work of Heaven;   10
Considering duly that a prince's court
Is like a common fountain, whence should flow
Pure silver drops in general, but if't chance
Some cursed example poison't near the head,
Death and diseases through the whole land spread.   15
And what is't makes this blessed government
But a most provident council, who dare freely
Inform him the corruption of the times?
Though some o' th' court hold it presumption
To instruct princes what they ought to do,   20
It is a noble duty to inform them
What they ought to foresee. Here comes Bosola,

7 **quits** rids 9 **which** the king's action 18 **inform** inform of

1

The only court-gall; yet I observe his railing
Is not for simple love of piety.
25 Indeed, he rails at those things which he wants;
Would be as lecherous, covetous, or proud,
Bloody, or envious, as any man,
If he had means to be so. Here's the Cardinal.

(*Enter the* CARDINAL *and* BOSOLA)

BOSOLA.   I do haunt you still.
30 CARDINAL.   So.
BOSOLA.   I have done you better service than to be
slighted thus. Miserable age, where only the reward of
doing well is the doing of it!
CARDINAL.   You enforce your merit too much.
35 BOSOLA.   I fell into the galleys in your service; where,
for two years together, I wore two towels instead of a
shirt, with a knot on the shoulder, after the fashion of
a Roman mantle. Slighted thus? I will thrive some way.
Blackbirds fatten best in hard weather; why not I in
40 these dog-days?
CARDINAL.   Would you could become honest!
BOSOLA.   With all your divinity do but direct me the
way to it. I have known many travel far for it, and yet
return as arrant knaves as they went forth, because they
45 carried themselves always along with them. (*Exit* CAR-
DINAL) Are you gone? Some fellows, they say, are possessed with the devil, but this great fellow were able to
possess the greatest devil, and make him worse.
ANTONIO.   He hath denied thee some suit?
50 BOSOLA.   He and his brother are like plum-trees that
grow crooked over standing-pools; they are rich and
o'er-laden with fruit, but none but crows, pies, and
caterpillars feed on them. Could I be one of their
flattering panders, I would hang on their ears like a
55 horseleech till I were full and then drop off. I pray,
leave me. Who would rely upon these miserable de-
pendencies, in expectation to be advanced tomorrow?

23 **gall** morbid growth on plants 36 **towels** rags 43-45 **I
have known . . . them** the idea borrowed from Montaigne's
Essays 51 **standing-pools** pools covered with green scum

What creature ever fed worse than hoping **Tantalus?**
Nor ever died any man more fearfully than he that
hoped for a pardon. There are rewards for hawks and 60
dogs when they have done us service; but for a soldier
that hazards his limbs in a battle, nothing but a kind of
geometry in his last supportation.

DELIO. Geometry?

BOSOLA. Aye, to hang in a fair pair of slings, take 65
his latter swing in the world upon an honorable pair
of crutches, from hospital to hospital. Fare ye well, sir:
and yet do not you scorn us; for places in the court
are but like beds in the hospital, where this man's head
lies at that man's foot, and so lower and lower. (*Exit*) 70

DELIO. I knew this fellow seven years in the galleys
For a notorious murder; and 'twas thought
The Cardinal suborned it. He was released
By the French general, Gaston de Foix,
When he recovered Naples.

ANTONIO.   'Tis great pity 75
He should be thus neglected; I have heard
He 's very valiant. This foul melancholy
Will poison all his goodness; for, I'll tell you,
If too immoderate sleep be truly said
To be an inward rust unto the soul, 80
It then doth follow want of action
Breeds all black malcontents; and their close rearing,
Like moths in cloth, do hurt for want of wearing.

DELIO. The presence 'gins to fill: you promised me
To make me the partaker of the natures 85
Of some of your great courtiers.

ANTONIO.   The Lord Cardinal's,
And other strangers that are now in court?
I shall. Here comes the great Calabrian duke.

(*Enter* FERDINAND, CASTRUCCIO, SILVIO, RODERIGO,
GRISOLAN, *and Attendants*)

FERDINAND. Who took the ring oftenest?

58 **Tantalus** a son of Zeus, condemned to eternal hunger and
thirst in the presence of food and water 63 **geometry . . .
supportation** a pair of crutches his only support 89 **Who
. . . oftenest** who most often caught on his lance a ring
suspended in the air

90 SILVIO. Antonio Bologna, my lord.

FERDINAND. Our sister duchess' great-master of her household? Give him the jewel. When shall we leave this sportive action, and fall to action indeed?

CASTRUCCIO. Methinks, my lord, you should not
95 desire to go to war in person.

FERDINAND. Now for some gravity. Why, my lord?

CASTRUCCIO. It is fitting a soldier arise to be a prince, but not necessary a prince descend to be a captain.

100 FERDINAND. No?

CASTRUCCIO. No, my lord, he were far better do it by a deputy.

FERDINAND. Why should he not as well sleep or eat by a deputy? This might take idle, offensive, and base
105 office from him, whereas the other deprives him of honor.

CASTRUCCIO. Believe my experience, that realm is never long in quiet where the ruler is a soldier.

FERDINAND. Thou told'st me thy wife could not
110 endure fighting.

CASTRUCCIO. True, my lord.

FERDINAND. And of a jest she broke of a captain she met full of wounds. I have forgot it.

CASTRUCCIO. She told him, my lord, he was a piti-
115 ful fellow, to lie, like the children of Ismael, all in tents.

FERDINAND. Why, there's a wit were able to undo all the chirurgeons o' the city; for although gallants should quarrel and had drawn their weapons and were
120 ready to go to it, yet her persuasions would make them put up.

CASTRUCCIO. That she would, my lord.

FERDINAND. How do you like my Spanish gennet?

RODERIGO. He is all fire.

125 FERDINAND. I am of Pliny's opinion, I think he was

112 **broke of** told concerning 116 **tents** a pun on lint bandages 118 **chirurgeons** surgeons 123 **gennet** a small horse
125 **Pliny** a Roman writer on natural history

begot by the wind; he runs as if he were ballassed
with quick-silver.

SILVIO.   True, my lord, he reels from the tilt often.

RODERIGO *and* GRISOLAN.   Ha, ha, ha!

FERDINAND.   Why do you laugh? Methinks, you that **130**
are courtiers should be my touchwood, take fire when
I give fire; that is, laugh [but] when I laugh, were the
subject never so witty.

CASTRUCCIO.   True, my lord. I myself have heard
a very good jest, and have scorned to seem to have **135**
so silly a wit as to understand it.

FERDINAND.   But I can laugh at your fool, my lord.

CASTRUCCIO.   He cannot speak, you know, but he
makes faces: my lady cannot abide him.

FERDINAND.   No?   **140**

CASTRUCCIO.   Nor endure to be in merry company,
for she says too much laughing and too much company
fills her too full of the wrinkle.

FERDINAND.   I would, then, have a mathematical instrument made for her face, that she might not laugh **145**
out of compass. I shall shortly visit you at Milan,
Lord Silvio.

SILVIO.   Your Grace shall arrive most welcome.

FERDINAND.   You are a good horseman, Antonio.
You have excellent riders in France. What do you **150**
think of good horsemanship?

ANTONIO.   Nobly, my lord: as out of the Grecian
horse issued many famous princes, so out of brave
horsemanship arise the first sparks of growing resolu-
tion that raise the mind to noble action.   **155**

FERDINAND.   You have bespoke it worthily.

SILVIO.   Your brother, the Lord Cardinal, and sister
duchess.

(*Re-enter* CARDINAL, *with* DUCHESS, CARIOLA,
and JULIA)

CARDINAL.   Are the galleys come about?

126 **ballassed** ballasted   131 **touchwood** wood used for tinder
152 **Grecian horse** the artificial horse that concealed **the**
Greek warriors invading Troy

GRISOLAN.   They are, my lord.
160 FERDINAND.   Here's the Lord Silvio is come to take
     his leave.
     DELIO.   Now, sir, your promise. What's that Car-
         dinal?
I mean his temper? They say he's a brave fellow,
Will play his five thousand crowns at tennis, dance,
Court ladies, and one that hath fought single combats.
165 ANTONIO.   Some such flashes superficially hang on
him for form; but observe his inward character: he is
a melancholy churchman; the spring in his face is nothing but the engendering of toads; where he is jealous
of any man, he lays worse plots for them than ever
170 was imposed on Hercules, for he strews in his way
flatter[er]s, panders, intelligencers, atheists, and a
thousand such political monsters. He should have been
Pope; but instead of coming to it by the primitive de-
cency of the Church, he did bestow bribes so largely
175 and so impudently as if he would have carried it away
without Heaven's knowledge. Some good he hath
done——
     DELIO.   You have given too much of him. What's
         his brother?
     ANTONIO.   The duke there? A most perverse and
         turbulent nature.
180 What appears in him mirth is merely outside;
If he laughs heartily, it is to laugh
All honesty out of fashion.
     DELIO.   Twins?
     ANTONIO.   In quality.
He speaks with others' tongues, and hears men's suits
With others' ears; will seem to sleep o' th' bench
185 Only to entrap offenders in their answers;
Dooms men to death by information;
Rewards by hearsay.
     DELIO.   Then the law to him
Is like a foul black cobweb to a spider:

163 **play** wager 168 **engendering of toads** a symbol of the
loathsomely ugly 172 **political** intriguing 186 **information**
the reports of paid informers

He makes [of] it his dwelling and a prison
To entangle those shall feed him.
   ANTONIO.   Most true: 190
He never pays debts unless they be shrewd turns,
And those he will confess that he doth owe.
Last, for his brother there, the Cardinal,
They that do flatter him most say oracles
Hang at his lips; and verily I believe them,   195
For the devil speaks in them.
But for their sister, the right noble duchess,
You never fixed your eye on three fair medals
Cast in one figure, of so different temper.
For her discourse, it is so full of rapture,   200
You only will begin then to be sorry
When she doth end her speech, and wish, in wonder,
She held it less vain-glory to talk much,
Than your penance to hear her: whilst she speaks,
She throws upon a man so sweet a look,   205
That it were able [to] raise one to a galliard
That lay in a dead palsy, and to dote
On that sweet countenance; but in that look
There speaketh so divine a continence
As cuts off all lascivious and vain hope.   210
Her days are practised in such noble virtue
That sure her nights, nay, more, her very sleeps,
Are more in heaven than other ladies' shrifts.
Let all sweet ladies break their flattering glasses,
And dress themselves in her.
   DELIO.   Fie, Antonio,   215
You play the wire-drawer with her commendations.
   ANTONIO.   I'll case the picture up: only thus much;
All her particular worth grows to this sum,
She stains the time past, lights the time to come.
   CARDINAL.   You must attend my lady in the gallery, 220
Some half an hour hence.
   ANTONIO.   I shall.
                     (*Exeunt* ANTONIO *and* DELIO)

200-204 **For her discourse . . . hear her** idea and some
phrases from Pettie's translation of Guazzo's *Civil Conversa-
tion* 216 **You play . . . commendations** you spin out her
praises 219 **stains** deprives of lustre

FERDINAND. Sister, I have a suit to you.
DUCHESS.   To me, sir?
FERDINAND. A gentleman here, Daniel de Bosola,
One that was in the galleys—
DUCHESS.   Yes, I know him.
FERDINAND. A worthy fellow he is. Pray, let me
225   entreat for
The provisorship of your horse.
DUCHESS.   Your knowledge of him
Commends him and prefers him.
FERDINAND.   Call him hither.
                              (*Exit Attendant*)
We [are] now upon parting. Good Lord Silvio,
Do us commend to all our noble friends
At the leaguer.
SILVIO.   Sir, I shall.
230   DUCHESS.   You are for Milan?
SILVIO. I am.
DUCHESS. Bring the caroches. We'll bring you down
To the haven.   (*Exeunt all but* FERDINAND *and
                              the* CARDINAL)
CARDINAL. Be sure you entertain that Bosola
235 For your intelligence: I would not be seen in 't;
And therefore many times I have slighted him
When he did court our furtherance, as this morning.
FERDINAND. Antonio, the great-master of her house-
    hold.
Had been far fitter.
CARDINAL.   You are deceived in him:
240 His nature is too honest for such business.
He comes: I'll leave you.   (*Exit*)

(*Re-enter* BOSOLA)

BOSOLA.   I was lured to you.
FERDINAND. My brother, here, the Cardinal could
    never
Abide you.

230 **leaguer** camp 232 **caroches** coaches 235 **intelligence** information gathered by a paid informer 241 **lured** a meta-
phor from falconry

BOSOLA.   Never since he was in my debt.

FERDINAND.   Maybe some oblique character in your
    face

Made him suspect you.

BOSOLA.   Doth he study physiognomy?   245

There's no more credit to be given to th' face

Than to a sick man's urine, which some call

The physician's whore because she cozens him.

He did suspect me wrongfully.

FERDINAND.   For that

You must give great men leave to take their times.   250

Distrust doth cause us seldom be deceived:

You see, the oft shaking of the cedar-tree

Fastens it more at root.

BOSOLA.   Yet, take heed;

For to suspect a friend unworthily

Instructs him the next way to suspect you,   255

And prompts him to deceive you.

FERDINAND.   (*Giving him money*) There's gold.

BOSOLA.   So:

What follows? Never rained such showers as these

Without thunderbolts i' th' tail of them. Whose throat
    must I cut?

FERDINAND.   Your inclination to shed blood rides
    post

Before my occasion to use you. I give you that   260

To live i' th' court here, and observe the duchess;

To note all the particulars of her havior,

What suitors do solicit her for marriage,

And whom she best affects. She's a young widow:

I would not have her marry again.

BOSOLA.   No, sir?   265

FERDINAND.   Do not you ask the reason, but be satis-
    fied

I say I would not.

BOSOLA.   It seems you would create me

One of your familiars.

FERDINAND.   Familiar? What's that?

---

248 cozens deceives **264 affects** likes **268 familiars** evil
spirits

BOSOLA.   Why, a very quaint invisible devil in flesh,
An intelligencer.

270   FERDINAND.   Such a kind of thriving thing
I would wish thee, and ere long thou may'st arrive
At a higher place by 't.
          BOSOLA.   Take your devils,
Which hell calls angels; these cursed gifts would make
You a corrupter, me an impudent traitor;

275 And should I take these, they'd take me [to] hell.
          FERDINAND.   Sir, I'll take nothing from you that I
                      have given:
There is a place that I procured for you
This morning, the provisorship o' th' horse;
Have you heard on 't?
          BOSOLA.   No.

280   FERDINAND.   'Tis yours. Is't not worth thanks?
          BOSOLA.   I would have you curse yourself now, that
                      your bounty,
Which makes men truly noble, e'er should make me
A villain. Oh, that to avoid ingratitude
For the good deed you have done me, I must do

285 All the ill man can invent! Thus the devil
Candies all sins o'er; and what heaven terms vile,
That names he complimental.
          FERDINAND.   Be yourself;
Keep your old garb of melancholy; 'twill express
You envy those that stand above your reach,

290 Yet strive not to come near 'em: this will gain
Access to private lodgings, where yourself
May, like a politic dormouse—
          BOSOLA.   As I have seen some
Feed in a lord's dish, half asleep, not seeming
To listen to any talk; and yet these rogues

295 Have cut his throat in a dream. What's my place?
The provisorship o' th' horse? Say, then, my corruption
Grew out of horse-dung. I am your creature.
          FERDINAND.   Away!
                                            (*Exit*)

273 angels a pun on gold coins   287 complimental admirable

BOSOLA.   Let good men, for good deeds, covet good
fame,
Since place and riches oft are bribes of shame:
Sometimes the devil doth preach.   (*Exit*)   **300**

SCENE II

(*Enter* FERDINAND, DUCHESS, CARDINAL, *and*
CARIOLA)

CARDINAL.   We are to part from you, and your own
discretion
Must now be your director.
FERDINAND.   You are a widow:
You know already what man is; and therefore
Let not youth, high promotion, eloquence—
CARDINAL.   No,
Nor any thing without the addition, honor,   **5**
Sway your high blood.
FERDINAND.   Marry! They are most luxurious
Will wed twice.
CARDINAL.   Oh, fie!
FERDINAND.   Their livers are more spotted
Than Laban's sheep.
DUCHESS.   Diamonds are of most value,
They say, that have passed through most jewellers'
hands.   **10**
FERDINAND.   Whores by that rule are precious.
DUCHESS.   Will you hear me?
I'll never marry.
CARDINAL.   So most widows say;
But commonly that motion lasts no longer
Than the turning of an hour-glass; the funeral sermon
And it end both together.
FERDINAND.   Now hear me: **15**
You live in a rank pasture, here, i' th' court;
There is a kind of honey-dew that's deadly;
'Twill poison your fame; look to't: be not cunning;
For they whose faces do belie their hearts

6 **luxurious** lascivious 9 **Laban's sheep** *Genesis.* xxx. 31-42
13 **motion** intention 17 **honey-dew** a sticky substance found
in certain plants

20 Are witches ere they arrive at twenty years,
    Aye, and give the devil suck.
        DUCHESS.   This is terrible good counsel.
        FERDINAND. Hypocrisy is woven of a fine small
            thread,
    Subtler than Vulcan's engine: yet, believe't,
    Your darkest actions, nay, your privatest thoughts,
    Will come to light.
25   CARDINAL.   You may flatter yourself,
    And take your own choice; privately be married
    Under the eaves of night—
        FERDINAND.   Think'st the best voyage
    That e'er you made; like the irregular crab,
    Which, though't goes backward, thinks that it goes right
30 Because it goes its own way; but observe,
    Such weddings may more properly be said
    To be executed than celebrated.
        CARDINAL.   The marriage night
    Is the entrance into some prison.
        FERDINAND.   And those joys,
    Those lustful pleasures, are like heavy sleeps
    Which do forerun man's mischief.
35   CARDINAL.   Fare you well.
    Wisdom begins at the end: remember it.   (*Exit*)
        DUCHESS.   I think this speech between you both was
            studied,
    It came so roundly off.
        FERDINAND.   You are my sister;
    This was my father's poniard, do you see?
40 I'd be loth to see 't look rusty, 'cause 'twas his.
    I would have you to give o'er these chargeable revels:
    A visor and a mask are whispering-rooms
    That were never built for goodness—fare ye well—
    And women like that part which, like the lamprey,
    Hath never a bone in 't.
        DUCHESS.   Fie, sir!
45   FERDINAND.   Nay,

23 **Vulcan's engine** the device contrived by Vulcan to trap
Mars and Venus

I mean the tongue; variety of courtship.
What cannot a neat knave with a smooth tale
Make a woman believe? Farewell, lusty widow. (*Exit*)
    DUCHESS.   Shall this move me? If all my royal kin-
       dred
Lay in my way unto this marriage,   **50**
I'd make them my low footsteps; and even now,
Even in this hate, as men in some great battles,
By apprehending danger, have achieved
Almost impossible actions (I have heard soldiers say
    so),
So I through frights and threatenings will assay   **55**
This dangerous venture. Let old wives report
I winked and chose a husband. Cariola,
To thy known secrecy I have given up
More than my life—my fame.
    CARIOLA.   Both shall be safe,
For I'll conceal this secret from the world   **60**
As warily as those that trade in poison
Keep poison from their children.
    DUCHESS.   Thy protestation
Is ingenious and hearty: I believe it.
Is Antonio come?
    CARIOLA.   He attends you.
    DUCHESS.   Good dear soul,
Leave me, but place thyself behind the arras,   **65**
Where thou mayst overhear us. Wish me good speed,
For I am going into a wilderness
Where I shall find nor path nor friendly clue
To be my guide.   (CARIOLA *goes behind the arras*)

               (*Enter* ANTONIO)

               I sent for you: sit down;
Take pen and ink, and write. Are you ready?
    ANTONIO.   **Yes.**   **70**
    DUCHESS.   What did I say?
    ANTONIO.   That I should write somewhat.

---

57 winked shut my eyes, i.e., chose blindly **63 ingenious and hearty** honest and heart-felt

DUCHESS.   Oh, I remember.
After these triumphs and this large expense,
It's fit, like thrifty husbands, we inquire
75 What's laid up for to-morrow.
    ANTONIO.   So please your beauteous excellence.
    DUCHESS.   Beauteous?
Indeed, I thank you: I look young for your sake;
You have ta'en my cares upon you.
    ANTONIO.   I'll fetch your grace
The particulars of your revenue and expense.
    DUCHESS.   Oh, you are an upright treasurer: but you
80   mistook;
For when I said I meant to make inquiry
What's laid up for to-morrow, I did mean
What's laid up yonder for me.
    ANTONIO.   Where?
    DUCHESS.   In heaven.
I am making my will (as 'tis fit princes should,
85 In perfect memory), and, I pray sir, tell me,
Were not one better make it smiling thus
Than in deep groans and terrible ghastly looks,
As if the gifts we parted with procured
That violent distraction?
    ANTONIO.   Oh, much better.
    DUCHESS.   If I had a husband now, this care were
90   quit:
But I intend to make you overseer.
What good deed shall we first remember? Say.
    ANTONIO.   Begin with that first good deed began i'
    th' world
After man's creation, the sacrament of marriage:
95 I'd have you first provide for a good husband;
Give him all.
    DUCHESS.   All?
    ANTONIO.   Yes, your excellent self.
    DUCHESS.   In a winding-sheet?
    ANTONIO.   In a couple.
    DUCHESS.   Saint Winfred, that were a strange will!

88 procured brought on **97 couple** pair of sheets **98 Saint Winfred** a Welsh virgin saint

ANTONIO.   'Twere strange[r] if there were no will
   in you
To marry again.
   DUCHESS.   What do you think of marriage?   100
   ANTONIO.   I take't, as those that deny purgatory;
It locally contains or Heaven or hell;
There's no third place in 't.
   DUCHESS.   How do you affect it?
   ANTONIO.   My banishment, feeling my melancholy,
Would often reason thus—
   DUCHESS.   Pray, let's hear it.   105
   ANTONIO.   Say a man never marry, nor have chil-
      dren,
What takes that from him? Only the bare name
Of being a father, or the weak delight
To see the little wanton ride a-cock-horse
Upon a painted stick, or hear him chatter   110
Like a taught starling.
   DUCHESS.   Fie, fie, what's all this?
One of your eyes is blood-shot; use my ring to 't,
They say 'tis very sovereign. 'Twas my wedding-ring,
And I did vow never to part with it
But to my second husband.
   ANTONIO.   You have parted with it now. 115
   DUCHESS.   Yes, to help your eyesight.
   ANTONIO.   You have made me stark blind.
   DUCHESS.   How?
   ANTONIO.   There is a saucy and ambitious devil
Is dancing in this circle.
   DUCHESS.   Remove him.
   ANTONIO.   How?
   DUCHESS.   There needs small conjuration, when your
      finger
May do it: this; is it fit?
      ([*She puts the ring upon his finger;*] *he kneels*)
   ANTONIO.   What said you?
   DUCHESS.   Sir,   120

103 affect fancy 113 sovereign effective 118 circle a pun on
the ring and the necromancer's circle formed to raise a devil

This goodly roof of yours is too low built;
I cannot stand upright in 't nor discourse,
Without I raise it higher: raise yourself;
Or, if you please, my hand to help you: so. (*Raises him*)
  ANTONIO. Ambition, madam, is a great man's mad-
125 ness,
That is not kept in chains and close-pent rooms,
But in fair lightsome lodgings, and is girt
With the wild noise of prattling visitants,
Which makes it lunatic beyond all cure.
130 Conceive not I am so stupid but I aim
Whereto your favors tend, but he's a fool
That, being a-cold, would thrust his hands i' th' fire
To warm them.
  DUCHESS. So, now the ground's broke,
You may discover what a wealthy mine
I make you lord of.
135 ANTONIO. O my unworthiness!
  DUCHESS. You were ill to sell yourself:
This darkening of your worth is not like that
Which tradesmen use i' th' city, their false lights
Are to rid bad wares off, and I must tell you,
140 If you will know where breathes a complete man
(I speak it without flattery), turn your eyes,
And progress through yourself.
  ANTONIO.   Were there nor heaven
Nor hell, I should be honest: I have long served virtue,
And ne'er ta'en wages of her.
  DUCHESS. Now she pays it.
145 The misery of us that are born great!
We are forced to woo, because none dare woo us;
And as a tyrant doubles with his words
And fearfully equivocates, so we
Are forced to express our violent passions
150 In riddles and in dreams, and leave the path
Of simple virtue, which was never made
To seem the thing it is not. Go, go brag

121 **roof** head as she looks down on him   130 **aim** guess   136
ill . . . yourself a poor salesman   137 **darkening** dimming of
lights to conceal the inferiority of merchandise   147 **doubles
. . . words** uses words with a double meaning

You have left me heartless; mine is in your bosom:
I hope 'twill multiply love there. You do tremble:
Make not your heart so dead a piece of flesh,   155
To fear more than to love me. Sir, be confident:
What is 't distracts you? This is flesh and blood, sir;
'Tis not the figure cut in alabaster
Kneels at my husband's tomb. Awake, awake, man!
I do here put off all vain ceremony,   160
And only do appear to you a young widow
That claims you for her husband, and, like a widow,
I use but half a blush in 't.
 ANTONIO.   Truth speak for me;
I will remain the constant sanctuary
Of your good name.
 DUCHESS.   I thank you, gentle love: 165
And 'cause you shall not come to me in debt,
Being now my steward, here upon your lips
I sign your *Quietus est*. This you should have begged
  now:
I have seen children oft eat sweetmeats thus,
As fearful to devour them too soon.   170
 ANTONIO. But for your brothers?
 DUCHESS.   Do not think of them.
All discord without this circumference
Is only to be pitied, and not feared;
Yet, should they know it, time will easily
Scatter the tempest.
 ANTONIO. These words should be mine,   175
And all the parts you have spoke, if some part of it
Would not have savoured flattery.
 DUCHESS.   Kneel.
   (CARIOLA *comes from behind the arras*)
 ANTONIO.   Ha!
 DUCHESS. Be not amazed; this woman's of my
  counsel:
I have heard lawyers say, a contract in a chamber
Per verba [*de*] *presenti* is absolute marriage.   180
     (*She and* ANTONIO *kneel*)

168 Quietus est final settlement of an account 180 Per . . .
presenti by words in the present tense, referring to the "I
take thee" of the marriage ceremony

Bless, heaven, this sacred gordian, which let violence
Never untwine!
    ANTONIO.   And may our sweet affections, like the
       spheres,
Be still in motion!
    DUCHESS.   Quickening, and make
185 The like soft music!
    ANTONIO.   That we may imitate the loving palms,
Best emblem of a peaceful marriage, that ne'er
Bore fruit, divided!
    DUCHESS.   What can the Church force more?
    ANTONIO.   That fortune may not know an accident,
190 Either of joy or sorrow, to divide
Our fixèd wishes!
    DUCHESS.   How can the Church build faster?
We now are man and wife, and 'tis the Church
That must but echo this. Maid, stand apart:
I now am blind.
    ANTONIO.   What's your conceit in this?
    DUCHESS.   I would have you lead your fortune by
195   the hand
Unto your marriage bed
(You speak in me this, for we now are one);
We'll only lie, and talk together, and plot
To appease my humorous kindred; and if you please,
200 Like the old tale in "Alexander and Lodowick,"
Lay a naked sword between us, keep us chaste.
Oh, let me shroud my blushes in your bosom,
Since 'tis the treasury of all my secrets!
                (*Exeunt* DUCHESS *and* ANTONIO)
    CARIOLA.   Whether the spirit of greatness or of
     woman
205 Reign most in her, I know not; but it shows
A fearful madness: I owe her much of pity.   (*Exit*)

181 **gordian** knot   184 **still** always   191 **faster** more solidly
194 **conceit** notion   200 **Alexander and Lodowick** a ballad
about two indistinguishable friends and one's impersonation
of the other to the wife of the first

Act II

Scene I

(Enter Bosola *and* Castruccio*)*

Bosola.   You say you would fain be taken for an
eminent courtier?

Castruccio.   'Tis the very main of my ambition.

Bosola.   Let me see: you have a reasonable good
face for 't already, and your nightcap expresses your 5
ears sufficient largely. I would have you learn to twirl
the strings of your band with a good grace, and in a
set speech, at th' end of every sentence, to hum three
or four times, or blow your nose till it smart again, to
recover your memory. When you come to be a presi- 10
dent in criminal causes, if you smile upon a prisoner,
hang him, but if you frown upon him and threaten
him, let him be sure to 'scape the gallows.

Castruccio.   I would be a very merry president.

Bosola.   Do not sup o' night; 'twill beget you an 15
admirable wit.

Castruccio.   Rather it would make me have a good
stomach to quarrel; for they say, your roaring boys eat
meat seldom, and that makes them so valiant. But how
shall I know whether the people take me for an emi- 20
nent fellow?

Bosola.   I will teach a trick to know it: give out
you lie a-dying, and if you hear the common people

3 **main** height   18 **stomach to** appetite for   **roaring boys**
rowdies

curse you, be sure you are taken for one of the prime
25 nightcaps.

(*Enter an* OLD LADY)

You come from painting now.

    OLD LADY.   From what?

    BOSOLA.   Why, from your scurvy face-physic. To
behold thee not painted inclines somewhat near a mira-
30 cle; these in thy face here were deep ruts and foul
sloughs the last progress. There was a lady in France
that, having had the small-pox, flayed the skin off her
face to make it more level; and whereas before she
looked like a nutmeg-grater, after she resembled an
35 abortive hedgehog.

    OLD LADY.   Do you call this painting?

    BOSOLA.   No, no, but you call [it] careening of an
old morphewed lady, to make her disembogue again:
there's rough-cast phrase to your plastic.

40   OLD LADY.   It seems you are well acquainted with
my closet.

    BOSOLA.   One would suspect it for a shop of witch-
craft, to find in it the fat of serpents, spawn of snakes,
Jews' spittle, and their young children's ordure; and all
45 these for the face. I would sooner eat a dead pigeon
taken from the soles of the feet of one sick of the
plague than kiss one of you fasting. Here are two of
you, whose sin of your youth is the very patrimony of
the physician; makes him renew his foot-cloth with the
50 spring, and change his high-priced courtezan with the
fall of the leaf. I do wonder you do not loathe your-
selves. Observe my meditation now.

What thing is in this outward form of man

25 **nightcaps** slang term for skull-caps worn by Sergeaunts at
Law 31 **lady in France** an illustration borrowed from Montaigne's *Essays* 37 **careening** scraping a ship before painting
38 **morphewed** scaly-skinned 38 **disembogue** put to sea 39
roughcast . . . plastic cheap plaster in return for your face-
modelling 42-44 **witchcraft . . . ordure** horrid details borrowed from Tofte's translation of Ariosto's *Satires* 45-47
pigeon . . . plague a regular treatment for the plague 47
fasting supposed to produce bad breath 49 **foot-cloth** trap-
pings of a horse

To be beloved? We account it ominous,
If nature do produce a colt, or lamb,   **55**
A fawn, or goat, in any limb resembling
A man, and fly from 't as a prodigy:
Man stands amazed to see his deformity
In any other creature but himself.
But in our own flesh, though we bear diseases   **60**
Which have their true names only ta'en from beasts—
As the most ulcerous wolf and swinish measle—
Though we are eaten up of lice and worms,
And though continually we bear about us
A rotten and dead body, we delight   **65**
To hide it in rich tissue: all our fear,
Nay, all our terror, is lest our physician
Should put us in the ground to be made sweet—
Your wife's gone to Rome: you two couple, and get
      you
To the wells at Lucca to recover your aches.   **70**
I have other work on foot.
                     (*Exeunt* CASTRUCCIO *and* OLD LADY)
                              I observe our duchess
Is sick a-days: she pukes, her stomach seethes,
The fins of her eye-lids look most teeming blue,
She wanes i' th' cheek, and waxes fat i' th' flank,
And, contrary to our Italian fashion,   **75**
Wears a loose-bodied gown: there's somewhat in 't.
I have a trick may chance discover it,
A pretty one; I have brought some apricocks,
The first our spring yields.

                  (*Enter* ANTONIO *and* DELIO)

   DELIO.   And so long since married?
You amaze me.
   ANTONIO.   Let me seal your lips for ever: **80**
For, did I think that anything but th' air
Could carry these words from you, I should wish
You had no breath at all. Now, sir, in your contempla-
      tion?
You are studying to become a great wise fellow?

62 **wolf** a skin disease **measle** a skin disease of swine 70
wells medicinal springs 78 **apricocks** old spelling of apricots

85   BOSOLA.   Oh, sir, the opinion of wisdom is a foul
     tetter that runs all over a man's body. If simplicity
     direct us to have no evil, it directs us to a happy being,
     for the subtlest folly proceeds from the subtlest wis-
     dom. Let me be simply honest.

     ANTONIO.   I do understand your inside.

90   BOSOLA.   Do you so?

     ANTONIO.   Because you would not seem to appear
     to th' world
     Puffed up with your preferment, you continue
     This out-of-fashion melancholy. Leave it, leave it.

     BOSOLA.   Give me leave to be honest in any phrase,
95   in any compliment whatsoever. Shall I confess myself
     to you? I look no higher than I can reach: they are the
     gods that must ride on winged horses. A lawyer's mule
     of a slow pace will both suit my disposition and busi-
     ness; for, mark me, when a man's mind rides faster than
100 his horse can gallop, they quickly both tire.

     ANTONIO.   You would look up to heaven, but I think
     The devil, that rules i' th' air, stands in your light.

     BOSOLA.   Oh, sir, you are lord of the ascendant,
     chief man with the duchess; a duke was your cousin-
105 german removed. Say you were lineally descended
     from King Pepin, or he himself, what of this? Search
     the heads of the greatest rivers in the world, you shall
     find them but bubbles of water. Some would think the
     souls of princes were brought forth by some more
110 weighty cause than those of meaner persons: they are
     deceived, there's the same hand to them; the like pas-
     sions sway them; the same reason that makes a vicar
     go to law for a tithe-pig, and undo his neighbours,
     makes them spoil a whole province, and batter down
115 goodly cities with the cannon.

                 (*Enter* DUCHESS *and Ladies*)

85-89 **opinion . . . honest** idea borrowed from Montaigne's
Essays 86 **tetter** skin disease 90 **inside** makeup 103 **lord of
the ascendant** in a favorable astrological position 106-115
Search . . . cannon ideas borrowed from Montaigne's *Essays* 113 **tithe-pig** pig offered as part of one's obligatory
offering

DUCHESS.　Your arm, Antonio; do I not grow fat?
I am exceeding short-winded. Bosola,
I would have you, sir, provide for me a litter,
Such a one as the Duchess of Florence rode in.
　　BOSOLA.　The duchess used one when she was great
　　　with child.　　　　　　　　　　　　　　　　　　120
　　DUCHESS.　I think she did. Come hither, mend my
　　　ruff;
Here, when?
Thou art such a tedious lady, and thy breath smells
Of lemon-peels. Would thou hadst done! Shall I swoon
Under thy fingers! I am so troubled　　　　　　　125
With the mother!
　　BOSOLA.　(*aside*) I fear too much.
　　DUCHESS.　　　　　　　　　I have heard you say
That the French courtiers wear their hats on 'fore
The king.
　　ANTONIO.　I have seen it.
　　DUCHESS.　　　　　　　In the presence?
　　ANTONIO.　　　　　　　　　　　　Yes.　　　130
　　DUCHESS.　Why should not we bring up that fashion?
　　　'Tis
Ceremony more than duty that consists
In the removing of a piece of felt.
Be you the example to the rest o' th' court;
Put on your hat first.
　　ANTONIO.　　　　You must pardon me.　　　135
I have seen, in colder countries than in France,
Nobles stand bare to th' prince, and the distinction
Methought showed reverently.
　　BOSOLA.　I have a present for your grace.
　　DUCHESS.　　　　　　　　　For me, sir?
　　BOSOLA.　Apricocks, madam.
　　DUCHESS.　　　　　　　O, sir, where are they?　140
I have heard of none to-year.
　　BOSOLA.　(*aside*)　　　Good; her color rises.
　　DUCHESS.　Indeed, I thank you: they are wondrous
　　　fair ones.

121 **mend my ruff** set my ruff straight　124 **lemon-peels** used
to sweeten the breath　126 **mother** hysteria, a meaning on
which Bosola immediately puns

What an unskillful fellow is our gardener!
We shall have none this month.

    BOSOLA.   Will not your grace pare them?

    DUCHESS.   No. They taste of musk, methinks; in-
145   deed they do.

    BOSOLA.   I know not: yet I wish your grace had
     pared 'em.

    DUCHESS.   Why?

    BOSOLA.   I forgot to tell you, the knave gardener,
Only to raise his profit by them the sooner,
Did ripen them in horse-dung.

    DUCHESS.   O, you jest.
You shall judge: pray taste one.

150   ANTONIO.   Indeed, madam,
I do not love the fruit.

    DUCHESS.   Sir, you are loath
To rob us of our dainties: 'tis a delicate fruit;
They say they are restorative.

    BOSOLA.   'Tis a pretty art,
This grafting.

155   DUCHESS.   'Tis so; a bettering of nature.

    BOSOLA.   To make a pippin grow upon a crab,
A damson on a blackthorn. (*aside*) How greedily she
    eats them!
A whirlwind strike off these bawd farthingales!
For, but for that and the loose-bodied gown,
160 I should have discovered apparently
The young springal cutting a caper in her belly.

    DUCHESS.   I thank you, Bosola. They were right
    good ones,
If they do not make me sick.

    ANTONIO.   How now, madam?

    DUCHESS.   This green fruit and my stomach are not
    friends;
165 How they swell me!

    BOSOLA.   (*aside*) Nay, you are too much swelled
    already.

    DUCHESS.   Oh, I am in an extreme cold sweat!

---

158 **bawd farthingales** loose-bodied gowns affected by Elizabethan prostitutes 161 **springal** stripling

BOSOLA. I am very sorry.

DUCHESS. Lights to my chamber! O good Antonio,
I fear I am undone!

DELIO. Lights there, lights!

(*Exeunt* DUCHESS *and Ladies. Exit, on the
other side,* BOSOLA)

ANTONIO. O my most trusty Delio, we are lost!   170
I fear she's fall'n in labor; and there's left
No time for her remove.

DELIO. Have you prepared
Those ladies to attend her? and procured
That politic safe conveyance for the midwife
Your duchess plotted?   175

ANTONIO. I have.

DELIO. Make use, then, of this forced occasion:
Give out that Bosola hath poisoned her
With these apricocks; that will give some color
For her keeping close.

ANTONIO. Fie, fie, the physicians
Will then flock to her.

DELIO. For that you may pretend   180
She'll use some prepared antidote of her own,
Lest the physicians should re-poison her.

ANTONIO. I am lost in amazement: I know not
   what to think on 't.   (*Ex[eunt]*)

SCENE II

(*Enter* BOSOLA)

BOSOLA. So, so, there's no question but her tetchi-
ness and most vulturous eating of the apricocks are
apparent signs of breeding.

(*Enter an* OLD LADY)

Now?

OLD LADY. I am in haste, sir.   5

BOSOLA. There was a young waiting-woman had a
monstrous desire to see the glass-house——

OLD LADY. Nay, pray let me go.

7 glass-house place where glass is blown

BOSOLA. And it was only to know what strange
10 instrument it was should swell up a glass to the fashion
of a woman's belly.

OLD LADY. I will hear no more of the glass-house.
You are still abusing women?

BOSOLA. Who, I? No; only, by the way now and
15 then, mention your frailties. The orange-tree bear[s]
ripe and green fruit and blossoms all together; and
some of you give entertainment for pure love, but more
for more precious reward. The lusty spring smells well,
but drooping autumn tastes well. If we have the same
20 golden showers that rained in the time of Jupiter the
thunderer, you have the same Danaës still, to hold up
their laps to receive them. Didst thou never study the
mathematics?

OLD LADY. What's that, sir?

25 BOSOLA. Why, to know the trick how to make a
many lines meet in one centre. Go, go, give your foster-
daughters good counsel: tell them, that the devil takes
delight to hang at a woman's girdle, like a false rusty
watch, that she cannot discern how the time passes.

(*Exit* OLD LADY)

(*Enter* ANTONIO, DELIO, RODERIGO, *and* GRISOLAN)

ANTONIO. Shut up the court-gates.

30 RODERIGO.   Why, sir? what's the danger?

ANTONIO. Shut up the posterns presently, and call
All the officers o' th' court.

GRISOLAN.   I shall instantly. (*Exit*)

ANTONIO. Who keeps the key o' th' park gate?

RODERIGO.   Forobosco.

ANTONIO. Let him bring 't presently.

(*Re-enter* GRISOLAN *with* SERVANTS)

1 SERVANT. O, gentlemen o' the court, the foulest
35   treason!

BOSOLA. (*aside*) If that these apricocks should be
poisoned now,
Without my knowledge!

20-21 **Jupiter . . . Danaës** reference to Jupiter's wooing
Danaë in the form of a shower of gold

1 SERVANT.   There was taken even now
A Switzer in the duchess' bed chamber—
   2 SERVANT.   A Switzer?
   1 SERVANT.   With a pistol in his great cod-piece.
   BOSOLA.   Ha, ha, ha!
   1 SERVANT.   The cod-piece was the case for 't.
   2 SERVANT.   There was **40**
A cunning traitor: who would have searched his cod-
    piece?
   1 SERVANT.   True, if he had kept out of the ladies'
    chambers.
And all the moulds of his buttons were leaden bullets.
   2 SERVANT.   O wicked cannibal!
A fire-lock in 's cod-piece!
   1 SERVANT.   'Twas a French plot,   **45**
Upon my life.
   2 SERVANT.   To see what the devil can do!
   ANTONIO.   [Are] all the officers here?
   SERVANTS.   We are.
   ANTONIO.   Gentlemen,
We have lost much plate you know, and but this evening
Jewels, to the value of four thousand ducats,   **50**
Are missing in the duchess' cabinet.
Are the gates shut?
   SERVANT.   Yes.
   ANTONIO.   'Tis the duchess' pleasure
Each officer be locked into his chamber
Till the sun-rising; and to send the keys
Of all their chests and of their outward doors   **55**
Into her bed-chamber. She is very sick.
   RODERIGO.   At her pleasure.
   ANTONIO.   She entreats you take 't not ill:
The innocent shall be the more approved by it.
   BOSOLA.   Gentlemen o' th' wood-yard, where's your
    Switzer now?
   1 SERVANT.   By this hand, 'twas credibly reported by
    one o' th' black guard.   **60**
        (*Exeunt all except* ANTONIO *and* DELIO)

38 **Switzer** a Swiss mercenary soldier 39 **cod-piece** an ap-
pendage to the tight hose worn by men 60 **black guard** scul-
lions

DELIO.   How fares it with the duchess?

ANTONIO.   She's exposed
Unto the worst of torture, pain, and fear.

DELIO.   Speak to her all happy comfort.

ANTONIO.   How I do play the fool with mine own
    danger!
65 You are this night, dear friend, to post to Rome;
My life lies in your service.

DELIO.   Do not doubt me.

ANTONIO.   Oh, 'tis far from me, and yet fear presents
    me
Somewhat that looks like danger.

DELIO.   Believe it,
'Tis but the shadow of your fear, no more;
70 How superstitiously we mind our evils!
The throwing down salt, or crossing of a hare,
Bleeding at nose, the stumbling of a horse,
Or singing of a cricket, are of power
To daunt whole man in us. Sir, fare you well:
75 I wish you all the joys of a blessed father:
And, for my faith, lay this unto your breast,
Old friends, like old swords, still are trusted best.
                             (*Exit*)

(*Enter* CARIOLA)

CARIOLA.   Sir, you are the happy father of a son:
Your wife commends him to you.

ANTONIO.   Blessed comfort!
80 For Heaven's sake tend her well: I'll presently
Go set a figure for 's nativity.   (*Exeunt*)

SCENE III

(*Enter* BOSOLA, *with a dark lantern*)

BOSOLA.   Sure I did hear a woman shriek: list, ha!
And the sound came, if I received it right,
From the duchess' lodgings. There's some stratagem
In the confining all our courtiers
5 To their several wards: I must have part of it;

81 set . . . nativity cast his horoscope

My intelligence will freeze else. List, again!
It may be 'twas the melancholy bird,
Best friend of silence and of solitariness,
The owl, that screamed so. Ha! Antonio?

(*Enter* ANTONIO *with a candle, his sword drawn*)

ANTONIO.   I heard some noise. Who's there? What
  art thou? Speak.   **10**
  BOSOLA.   Antonio? Put not your face nor body
To such a forced expression of fear.
I am Bosola, your friend.
  ANTONIO.   Bosola!
(*aside*) This mole does undermine me. Heard you not
A noise even now?
  BOSOLA.   From whence?
  ANTONIO.   From the duchess' lodging. **15**
  BOSOLA.   Not I. Did you?
  ANTONIO.   I did, or else I dreamed.
  BOSOLA.   Let's walk towards it.
  ANTONIO.   No, it may be 'twas
But the rising of the wind.
  BOSOLA.   Very likely.
Methinks 'tis very cold, and yet you sweat:
You look wildly.
  ANTONIO.   I have been setting a figure   **20**
For the duchess' jewels.
  BOSOLA.   Ah, and how falls your question?
Do you find it radical?
  ANTONIO.   What's that to you?
'Tis rather to be questioned what design,
When all men were commanded to the lodgings,
Makes you a night-walker.
  BOSOLA.   In sooth, I'll tell you: **25**
Now all the court's asleep, I thought the devil
Had least to do here; I came to say my prayers;
And if it do offend you I do so,
You are a fine courtier.
  ANTONIO.   (*aside*) This fellow will undo me.   **30**

20 setting a figure making an astrological calculation 22
radical an astrological term

You gave the duchess apricocks to-day:
Pray Heaven they were not poisoned!
    BOSOLA.   Poisoned? A Spanish fig
For the imputation!
    ANTONIO.   Traitors are ever confident
Till they are discovered. There were jewels stol'n, too;
35 In my conceit, none are to be suspected
More than yourself.
    BOSOLA.   You are a false steward.
    ANTONIO.   Saucy slave, I'll pull thee up by the roots.
    BOSOLA.   Maybe the ruin will crush you to pieces.
    ANTONIO.   You are an impudent snake indeed, sir:
40 Are you scarce warm, and do you show your sting?
You libel well, sir.
    BOSOLA.   No, sir: copy it out,
And I will set my hand to't.
    ANTONIO. (*aside*)   My nose bleeds.
One that were superstitious would count
This ominous, when it merely comes by chance:
45 Two letters, that are wrought here for my name,
Are drowned in blood!
Mere accident. For you, sir, I'll take order
I' th' morn you shall be safe: (*aside*) 'tis that must color
Her lying-in: sir, this door you pass not:
50 I do not hold it fit that you come near
The duchess' lodgings, till you have quit yourself.
(*aside*) The great are like the base, nay, they are the
    same,
When they seek shameful ways to avoid shame. (*Ex*[*it*])
    BOSOLA.   Antonio hereabout did drop a paper:
Some of your help, false friend: (*Opening his lantern*)
55   Oh, here it is.
What's here? A child's nativity calculated?
    'The duchess was delivered of a son, 'tween the hours
twelve and one in the night, *Anno Dom.* 1504,' that's
this year—'*decimo nono Decembris*,'—that's this night,
60 —'taken according to the meridian of Malfi,'—that's

32 **Spanish fig** an indecent gesture with the fingers 35 **conceit** opinion 40 **scarce warm** new in your position 41 **libel** defame, which Bosola punningly interprets as bring a formal charge in writing 55 **false friend** dark lantern

our duchess: happy discovery! 'The lord of the first
house being combust in the ascendant, signifies short
life; and Mars being in a human sign, joined to the tail
of the Dragon, in the eighth house, doth threaten a
violent death. *Caetera non scrutantur.*'   65
Why, now 'tis most apparent: this precise fellow
Is the duchess' bawd: I have it to my wish!
This is a parcel of intelligency
Our courtiers were cased up for: it needs must follow
That I must be committed on pretence   70
Of poisoning her; which I'll endure, and laugh at.
If one could find the father now! But that
Time will discover. Old Castruccio
I' th' morning posts to Rome: by him I'll send
A letter that shall make her brothers' galls   75
O'erflow their livers. This was a thrifty way.
Though lust do mask in ne'er so strange disguise,
She's oft found witty, but is never wise.   (*Exit*)

Scene IV

(*Enter* Cardinal *and* Julia)

CARDINAL.   Sit. Thou art my best of wishes. Prithee,
    tell me
What trick didst thou invent to come to Rome
Without thy husband.
    JULIA.   Why, my lord, I told him
I came to visit an old anchorite
Here for devotion.
    CARDINAL.   Thou art a witty false one,   5
I mean, to him.
    JULIA.   You have prevailed with me
Beyond my strongest thoughts! I would not now
Find you inconstant.
    CARDINAL.   Do not put thyself
To such a voluntary torture, which proceeds
Out of your own guilt.
    JULIA.   How, my lord?

65 Caetera non scrutantur The other details were not in-
terpreted 4 anchorite a religious recluse

10   CARDINAL.   You fear
My constancy, because you have approved
Those giddy and wild turning[s] in yourself.
      JULIA.   Did you e'er find them?
      CARDINAL.   Sooth, generally for women;
A man might strive to make glass malleable,
Ere he should make them fixed.
15   JULIA.   So, my lord.
      CARDINAL.   We had need go borrow that fantastic
         glass
Invented by Galileo the Florentine
To view another spacious world i' th' moon,
And look to find a constant woman there.
      JULIA.   This is very well, my lord.
20   CARDINAL.   Why do you weep?
Are tears your justification? The self-same tears
Will fall into your husband's bosom, lady,
With a loud protestation that you love him
Above the world. Come, I'll love you wisely,
25 That's jealously, since I am very certain
You cannot make me cuckold.
      JULIA.   I'll go home
To my husband.
      CARDINAL.   You may thank me, lady,
I have taken you off your melancholy perch,
Bore you upon my fist, and showed you game,
30 And let you fly at it. I pray thee, kiss me.
When thou wast with thy husband, thou wast watched
Like a tame elephant: still you are to thank me:
Thou hadst only kisses from him and high feeding;
But what delight was that? 'Twas just like one
35 That hath a little fingering on the lute,
Yet cannot tune it: still you are to thank me.
      JULIA.   You told me of a piteous wound i' th' heart
And a sick liver, when you wooed me first,
And spake like one in physic.
      CARDINAL.   Who's that?
                  (*Enter* SERVANT)

11. **approved** experienced 16 **fantastic glass** telescope invented about 1609, here an anachronism 28-30 **perch . . .
fly** metaphors from falconry 39 **in physic** under treatment

Rest firm, for my affection to thee,   40
Lightning moves slow to 't.
    SERVANT.   Madam, a gentleman,
That's come post from Malfi, desires to see you.
    CARDINAL.   Let him enter. I'll withdraw.   (*Exit*)
    SERVANT.   He says
Your husband, old Castruccio, is come to Rome,
Most pitifully tired with riding post.   (*Exit*) 45

(*Enter* DELIO)

    JULIA.   Signior Delio! (*aside*) 'tis one of my old
    suitors.
    DELIO.   I was bold to come and see you.
    JULIA.   Sir, you are welcome.
    DELIO.   Do you lie here?
    JULIA.   Sure, your own experience
Will satisfy you no: our Roman prelates
Do not keep lodging for ladies.
    DELIO.   Very well.   50
I have brought you no commendations from your hus-
    band,
For I know none by him.
    JULIA.   I hear he's come to Rome.
    DELIO.   I never knew man and beast, of a horse and
    a knight,
So weary of each other: if he had had a good back,
He would have undertook to have borne his horse,   55
His breech was so pitifully sore.
    JULIA.   Your laughter
Is my pity.
    DELIO.   Lady, I know not whether
You want money, but I have brought you some.
    JULIA.   From my husband?
    DELIO.   No, from mine own allowance.
    JULIA.   I must hear the condition, ere I be bound to
    take it.   60
    DELIO.   Look on't, 'tis gold: hath it not a fine color?
    JULIA.   I have a bird more beautiful.

41 **to 't** in comparison to it 48 **lie** lodge 56-57 **Your laughter . . . pity** What arouses laughter in you arouses pity **in
me**

DELIO. Try the sound on 't.

JULIA.   A lute-string far exceeds it:
It hath no smell, like cassia or civet;
65 Nor is it physical, though some fond doctors
Persuade us seethe 't in cullises. I'll tell you,
This is a creature bred by——

(*Re-enter* SERVANT)

SERVANT.   Your husband's come,
Hath delivered a letter to the Duke of Calabria
That, to my thinking, hath put him out of his wits.
                                              (*Exit*)

70 JULIA. Sir, you hear:
Pray, let me know your business and your suit
As briefly as can be.

DELIO. With good speed: I would wish you,
At such time as you are non-resident
75 With your husband, my mistress.

JULIA. Sir, I'll go ask my husband if I shall,
And straight return your answer.   (*Exit*)

DELIO.   Very fine!
Is this her wit, or honesty, that speaks thus?
I heard one say the duke was highly moved
80 With a letter sent from Malfi. I do fear
Antonio is betrayed: how fearfully
Shows his ambition now! Unfortunate fortune!
They pass through whirlpools, and deep woes do shun,
Who the event weigh ere the action's done.   (*Exit*)

SCENE V

([*Enter*] CARDINAL, *and* FERDINAND *with a letter*)

FERDINAND. I have this night digged up a mandrake.

CARDINAL.   Say you?

FERDINAND. And I am grown mad with 't.

CARDINAL.   What's the prodigy?

---

65 **physical** restorative **fond** foolish 66 **seethe 't in cullises**
stew it in broths 82 **Shows** appears 1 **digged . . . mandrake** an action supposedly productive of madness

FERDINAND. Read there—a sister damned: she's
   loose i' th' hilts;
Grown a notorious strumpet.
   CARDINAL.   Speak lower.
   FERDINAND.   Lower?
Rogues do not whisper 't now, but seek to publish 't   5
(As servants do the bounty of their lords)
Aloud; and with a covetous searching eye,
To mark who note them. O, confusion seize her!
She hath had most cunning bawds to serve her turn,
And more secure conveyances for lust   10
Than towns of garrison for service.
   CARDINAL.   Is 't possible?
Can this be certain?
   FERDINAND.   Rhubarb, oh, for rhubarb
To purge this choler! Here's the cursèd day
To prompt my memory, and here 't shall stick
Till of her bleeding heart I make a sponge   15
To wipe it out.
   CARDINAL.   Why do you make yourself
So wild a tempest?
   FERDINAND.   Would I could be one,
That I might toss her palace 'bout her ears,
Root up her goodly forests, blast her meads,
And lay her general territory as waste   20
As she hath done her honors.
   CARDINAL.   Shall our blood,
The royal blood of Arragon and Castile,
Be thus attainted?
   FERDINAND.   Apply desperate physic:
We must not now use balsamum, but fire,
The smarting cupping-glass, for that 's the mean   25
To purge infected blood, such blood as hers.
There is a kind of pity in mine eye,
I'll give it to my handkercher; and now 'tis here,
I'll bequeath this to her bastard.
   CARDINAL.   What to do?

3 **loose i' th' hilts** unchaste   13 **cursèd day** a probable reference to the horoscope Bosola *has* turned over to him   25
cupping-glass device used for bleeding a patient

FERDINAND.   Why, to make soft lint for his mother's
30   wounds,
When I have hewed her to pieces.
CARDINAL.   Cursèd creature!
Unequal nature, to place women's hearts
So far upon the left side!
FERDINAND.   Foolish men,
That e'er will trust their honor in a bark
35   Made of so slight weak bulrush as is woman,
Apt every minute to sink it!
CARDINAL.   Thus ignorance, when it hath purchased
    honor,
It cannot wield it.
FERDINAND.   Methinks I see her laughing—
Excellent hyena! Talk to me somewhat, quickly,
40   Or my imagination will carry me
To see her in the shameful act of sin.
CARDINAL.   With whom?
FERDINAND.   Happily with some strong-thighed
    bargeman,
Or one [o'] the woodyard that can quoit the sledge
45   Or toss the bar, or else some lovely squire
That carries coals up to her privy lodgings.
CARDINAL.   You fly beyond your reason.
FERDINAND.   Go to, mistress!
'Tis not your whore's milk that shall quench my wild fire,
But your whore's blood.
CARDINAL.   How idly shows this rage, which carries
50   you,
As men conveyed by witches through the air,
On violent whirlwinds! This intemperate noise
Fitly resembles deaf men's shrill discourse,
Who talk aloud, thinking all other men
To have their imperfection.
55   FERDINAND.   Have not you
My palsy?
CARDINAL.   Yes, I can be angry, [but]
Without this rupture: there is not in nature

33 left side *Ecclesiastes*. x. 44 quoit the sledge throw the
hammer 57 **rupture** violent outbreak

A thing that makes man so deformed, so beastly,
As doth intemperate anger. Chide yourself.
You have divers men who never yet expressed   60
Their strong desire of rest but by unrest,
By vexing of themselves. Come, put yourself
In tune.
    FERDINAND.   So; I will only study to seem
The thing I am not. I could kill her now,
In you, or in myself; for I do think   65
It is some sin in us heaven doth revenge
By her.
    CARDINAL.   Are you stark mad?
    FERDINAND.   I would have their bodies
Burnt in a coal-pit with the ventage stopped,
That their cursed smoke might not ascend to heaven;
Or dip the sheets they lie in in pitch or sulphur,   70
Wrap them in 't, and then light them like a match;
Or else to-boil their bastard to a cullis,
And give 't his lecherous father to renew
The sin of his back.
    CARDINAL.   I'll leave you.
    FERDINAND.   Nay, I have done.
I am confident, had I been damned in hell,   75
And should have heard of this, it would have put me
Into a cold sweat. In, in; I'll go sleep.
Till I know who leaps my sister, I'll not stir:
That known, I'll find scorpions to string my whips,
And fix her in a general eclipse.   (*Exeunt*)   80

72 **to-boil** boil thoroughly 80 **eclipse** total eclipse, death

Act III

Scene I

(Enter Antonio *and* Delio*)*

ANTONIO.   Our noble friend, my most beloved Delio!
Oh, you have been a stranger long at court;
Came you along with the Lord Ferdinand?

    DELIO.   I did, sir. And how fares your noble duchess?

    ANTONIO.   Right fortunately well: she 's an excellent **5**
Feeder of pedigrees; since you last saw her,
She hath had two children more, a son and daughter.

    DELIO.   Methinks 'twas yesterday: let me but wink,
And not behold your face, which to mine eye
Is somewhat leaner, verily I should dream   **10**
It were within this half-hour.

    ANTONIO.   You have not been in law, friend Delio,
Nor in prison, nor a suitor at the court,
Nor begged the reversion of some great man's place,
Nor troubled with an old wife, which doth make   **15**
Your time so insensibly hasten.

    DELIO.   Pray, sir, tell me.
Hath not this news arrived yet to the ear
Of the lord cardinal?

    ANTONIO.   I fear it hath:
The Lord Ferdinand, that 's newly come to court,
Doth bear himself right dangerously.

    DELIO.   Pray, why?   **20**

    ANTONIO.   He is so quiet that he seems to sleep
The tempest out, as dormice do in winter.

16 insensibly without your being able to believe that time is
passing

Those houses that are haunted are most still
Till the devil be up.

    DELIO.   What say the common people?

25   ANTONIO.   The common rabble do directly say
She is a strumpet.

    DELIO.   And your graver heads
Which would be politic, what censure they?

    ANTONIO.   They do observe I grow to infinite pur-
        chase,
The left hand way, and all suppose the duchess
30 Would amend it, if she could; for, say they,
Great princes, though they grudge their officers
Should have such large and unconfinèd means
To get wealth under them, will not complain,
Lest thereby they should make them odious
35 Unto the people; for other obligation
Of love or marriage between her and me
They never dream of.

    DELIO.   The Lord Ferdinand
Is going to bed.

        (*Enter* DUCHESS, FERDINAND, *and* BOSOLA)

    FERDINAND.   I'll instantly to bed,
For I am weary. I am to bespeak
A husband for you.
40   DUCHESS.   For me, sir? Pray, who is 't?

    FERDINAND.   The great Count Malateste.

    DUCHESS.   Fie upon him!
A count? He 's a mere stick of sugar-candy;
You may look quite through him. When I choose
A husband, I will marry for your honor.

    FERDINAND.   You shall do well in 't. How is 't, worthy
45   Antonio?

    DUCHESS.   But, sir, I am to have private conference
    with you
About a scandalous report is spread
Touching mine honor.

    FERDINAND.   Let me be ever deaf to 't:

28 purchase wealth **29 The left hand way** illegitimately

One of Pasquil's paper bullets, court-calumny,
A pestilent air, which princes' palaces   50
Are seldom purged of. Yet, say that it were true,
I pour it in your bosom, my fixed love
Would strongly excuse, extenuate, nay, deny
Faults, were they apparent in you. Go, be safe
In your own innocency.
    DUCHESS.   (*aside*)   O blessèd comfort!   55
This deadly air is purged.
            (*Exeunt* [DUCHESS, ANTONIO, *and* DELIO])
    FERDINAND.   Her guilt treads on
Hot-burning coulters. Now, Bosola,
How thrives our intelligence?
    BOSOLA.   Sir, uncertainly
'Tis rumored she hath had three bastards, but
By whom we may go read i' th' stars.
    FERDINAND.   Why, some   60
Hold opinion all things are written there.
    BOSOLA.   Yes, if we could find spectacles to read
      them.
I do suspect there hath been some sorcery
Used on the duchess.
    FERDINAND.   Sorcery? To what purpose?
    BOSOLA.   To make her dote on some desertless fellow   65
She shames to acknowledge.
    FERDINAND.   Can your faith give way
To think there 's power in potions or in charms,
To make us love whether we will or no?
    BOSOLA.   Most certainly.
    FERDINAND.   Away! These are mere gulleries, horrid
      things,   70
Invented by some cheating mountebanks
To abuse us. Do you think that herbs or charms
Can force the will? Some trials have been made
In this foolish practice, but the ingredients
Were lenitive poisons, such as are of force   75
To make the patient mad; and straight the witch

49 **Pasquil's paper bullets** notorious popular satires initiated
by Pasquilla or Pasquino, a Roman cobbler   57 **coulters** iron
blades, used in mediaeval tests of chastity   70 **gulleries**
cheats   75 **lenitive** soothing but efficacious

Swears by equivocation they are in love.
The witchcraft lies in her rank blood. This night
I will force confession from her. You told me
80 You had got, within these two days, a false key
Into her bed-chamber.
    BOSOLA.   I have.
    FERDINAND.   As I would wish.
    BOSOLA.   What do you intend to do?
    FERDINAND.   Can you guess?
    BOSOLA.   No.
    FERDINAND.   Do not ask, then:
He that can compass me, and know my drifts,
85 May say he hath put a girdle 'bout the world,
And sounded all her quicksands.
    BOSOLA.   I do not
Think so.
    FERDINAND.   What do you think, then, pray?
    BOSOLA.   That you
Are your own chronicle too much, and grossly
Flatter yourself.
    FERDINAND.   Give me thy hand; I thank thee:
90 I never gave pension but to flatterers,
Till I entertained thee. Farewell.
That friend a great man's ruin strongly checks,
Who rails into his belief all his defects.   (*Exeunt*)

SCENE II

(*Enter* DUCHESS, ANTONIO, *and* CARIOLA)

    DUCHESS. Bring me the casket hither, and the glass.
You get no lodging here to-night, my lord.
    ANTONIO.   Indeed, I must persuade one.
    DUCHESS.   Very good:
I hope in time 'twill grow into a custom,
5 That noblemen shall come with cap and knee
To purchase a night's lodging of their wives.
    ANTONIO.   I must lie here.
    DUCHESS.   Must! You are a lord of misrule.

84 drifts plans 7 lord of misrule master of the Christmas revels

ANTONIO.   Indeed, my rule is only in the night.
DUCHESS.   To what use will you put me?
ANTONIO.   We'll sleep together.
DUCHESS.   Alas, what pleasure can two lovers find in
  sleep!   10
CARIOLA.   My lord, I lie with her often, and I know
She'll much disquiet you.
ANTONIO.   See, you are complained of.
CARIOLA.   For she's the sprawling'st bedfellow.
ANTONIO.   I shall like her
The better for that.
CARIOLA.   Sir, shall I ask you a question?
ANTONIO.   Oh, I pray thee, Cariola.
CARIOLA.   Wherefore still, when you lie 15
With my lady, do you rise so early?
ANTONIO.   Laboring men
Count the clock oftenest, Cariola, are glad
When their task's ended.
DUCHESS.   I'll stop your mouth. (*Kisses him*)
ANTONIO.   Nay, that's but one; Venus had two soft
  doves
To draw her chariot; I must have another—   20
                          (*She kisses him again*)
When wilt thou marry, Cariola?
CARIOLA.   Never, my lord.
ANTONIO.   Oh, fie upon this single life! Forgo it.
We read how Daphne, for her peevish flight,
Became a fruitless bay-tree; Syrinx turned
To the pale empty reed; Anaxarete   25
Was frozen into marble: whereas those
Which married, or proved kind unto their friends,
Were by a gracious influence transhaped
Into the olive, pomegranate, mulberry,
Became flowers, precious stones, or eminent stars. 30
CARIOLA.   This is a vain poetry, but I pray you tell
  me,
If there were proposed me, wisdom, riches, and beauty,
In three several young men, which should I choose?

24 Syrinx a nymph loved by Pan   25 Anaxarete whose lover
Iphis hanged himself when he failed to win her love

ANTONIO. 'Tis a hard question: this was Paris' case,
35 And he was blind in 't, and there was great cause;
For how was 't possible he could judge right,
Having three amorous goddesses in view,
And they stark naked? 'Twas a motion
Were able to benight the apprehension
40 Of the severest counsellor of Europe.
Now I look on both your faces so well formed,
It puts me in mind of a question I would ask.
    CARIOLA. What is 't?
    ANTONIO.   I do wonder why hard-favored ladies,
For the most part, keep worse-favored waiting-women
45 To attend them, and cannot endure fair ones.
    DUCHESS. Oh, that's soon answered.
Did you ever in your life know an ill painter
Desire to have his dwelling next door to the shop
Of an excellent picture-maker? 'Twould disgrace
50 His face-making, and undo him. I prithee,
When were we so merry? My hair tangles.
    ANTONIO. Pray thee, Cariola, let 's steal forth the room,
And let her talk to herself: I have divers times
Served her the like, when she hath chafed extremely.
55 I love to see her angry. Softly, Cariola.
                   (*Exeunt* [ANTONIO *and* CARIOLA])
    DUCHESS. Doth not the color of my hair 'gin to change?
When I wax grey, I shall have all the court
Powder their hair with arras, to be like me.
You have cause to love me; I entered you into my heart
60 Before you would vouchsafe to call for the keys.

           (*Enter* FERDINAND *behind*)

We shall one day have my brothers take you napping;
Methinks his presence, being now in court,
Should make you keep your own bed; but you'll say
Love mixed with fear is sweetest. I'll assure you,
65 You shall get no more children till my brothers

34 **Paris** son of the King of Troy, who was required to pass
judgment on the beauty of Juno, Pallas, and Aphrodite 38
motion sight 58 **arras** powdered orris-root

Consent to be your gossips. Have you lost your tongue?
'Tis welcome:
For know, whether I am doomed to live or die,
I can do both like a prince.
    FERDINAND.   Die, then, quickly!
                      (*Giving her a poniard*)
Virtue, where art thou hid? What hideous thing   **70**
Is it that doth eclipse thee?
    DUCHESS.   Pray, sir, hear me.
    FERDINAND.   Or is it true thou art but a bare name,
And no essential thing?
    DUCHESS.   Sir,—
    FERDINAND.   Do not speak.
    DUCHESS.   No, sir: I will plant my soul in mine ears,
      to hear you.
    FERDINAND.   O most imperfect light of human reason,   **75**
That mak'st [us] so unhappy to foresee
What we can least prevent! Pursue thy wishes,
And glory in them: there 's in shame no comfort
But to be past all bounds and sense of shame.
    DUCHESS.   I pray, sir, hear me. I am married.
    FERDINAND.   So!   **80**
    DUCHESS.   Happily, not to your liking: but for that,
Alas, your shears do come untimely now
To clip the bird's wings that 's already flown!
Will you see my husband?
    FERDINAND.   Yes, if I could change
Eyes with a basilisk.
    DUCHESS.   Sure, you came hither   **85**
By his confederacy.
    FERDINAND.   The howling of a wolf
Is music to thee, screech-owl: prithee, peace.
Whate'er thou art that hast enjoyed my sister,
For I am sure thou hear'st me, for thine own sake
Let me not know thee. I came hither prepared   **90**
To work thy discovery; yet am now persuaded
It would beget such violent effects

66 gossips friends 70-71 Virtue . . . thee 75-79 O most
. . . shame ideas and phrasing from Sidney's *Arcadia* 81
Happily perhaps 85 basilisk a fabulous monster, whose
glance brought death

As would damn us both. I would not for ten millions
I had beheld thee: therefore use all means
95 I never may have knowledge of thy name;
Enjoy thy lust still, and a wretched life,
On that condition. And for thee, vile woman,
If thou do wish thy lecher may grow old
In thy embracements, I would have thee build
100 Such a room for him as our anchorites
To holier use inhabit. Let not the sun
Shine on him till he 's dead; let dogs and monkeys
Only converse with him, and such dumb things
To whom nature denies use to sound his name;
105 Do not keep a paraquito, lest she learn it;
If thou do love him, cut out thine own tongue,
Lest it bewray him.

DUCHESS.   Why might not I marry?
I have not gone about in this to create
Any new world or custom.

FERDINAND.   Thou art undone;
110 And thou hast ta'en that massy sheet of lead
That hid thy husband's bones, and folded it
About my heart.

DUCHESS.   Mine bleeds for 't.

FERDINAND.   Thine? Thy heart?
What should I name 't unless a hollow bullet
Filled with unquenchable wild-fire?

DUCHESS.   You are in this
115 Too strict, and were you not my princely brother,
I would say, too wilful. My reputation
Is safe.

FERDINAND.   Dost thou know what reputation is?
I'll tell thee, to small purpose, since the instruction
120 Comes now too late.
Upon a time Reputation, Love, and Death,
Would travel o'er the world; and it was concluded
That they should part, and take three several ways.
Death told them, they should find him in great battles,
125 Or cities plagued with plagues. Love gives them counsel
To inquire for him 'mongst unambitious shepherds,

100 **room . . . anchorites** cell with only a small opening for
the passage of food and water to religious recluses

Where dowries were not talked of, and sometimes
'Mongst quiet kindred that had nothing left
By their dead parents. "Stay," quoth Reputation,
"Do not forsake me; for it is my nature,   130
If once I part from any man I meet,
I am never found again." And so for you:
You have shook hands with Reputation,
And made him invisible. So, fare you well.
I will never see you more.

DUCHESS.   Why should only I,   135
Of all the other princes of the world,
Be cased up, like a holy relic? I have youth
And a little beauty.

FERDINAND.   So you have some virgins
That are witches. I will never see thee more.   (*Exit*)

(*Enter* ANTONIO *with a Pistol,* [*and* CARIOLA])

DUCHESS.   You saw this apparition?

ANTONIO.   Yes. We are   140
Betrayed. How came he hither? I should turn
This to thee, for that.   (*Pointing the pistol at* CARIOLA)

CARIOLA.   Pray, sir, do; and when
That you have cleft my heart, you shall read there
Mine innocence.

DUCHESS.   That gallery gave him entrance.

ANTONIO.   I would this terrible thing would come
again,   145
That, standing on my guard, I might relate
My warrantable love.   (*She shows the poniard*)
               Ha! What means this?

DUCHESS.   He left this with me.

ANTONIO.   And it seems did wish
You would use it on yourself.

DUCHESS.   His action seemed
To intend so much.

ANTONIO.   This hath a handle to 't   150
As well as a point: turn it towards him, and
So fasten the keen edge in his rank gall.
                            (*Knocking within*)
How now! Who knocks? More earthquakes?

DUCHESS.   I stand

As if a mine beneath my feet were ready
To be blown up.
   CARIOLA.   'Tis Bosola.
155 DUCHESS.   Away!
O misery! Methinks unjust actions
Should wear these masks and curtains, and not we.
You must instantly part hence: I have fashioned it
Already.   (*Exit* ANTONIO)

(*Enter* BOSOLA)

   BOSOLA.   The duke your brother is ta'en up in a
160   whirlwind,
Hath took horse, and 's rid post to Rome.
   DUCHESS.   So late?
   BOSOLA.   He told me, as he mounted into th' saddle,
You were undone.
   DUCHESS.   Indeed, I am very near it.
   BOSOLA.   What 's the matter?
165 DUCHESS.   Antonio, the master of our household,
Hath dealt so falsely with me in 's accounts:
My brother stood engaged with me for money
Ta'en up of certain Neapolitan Jews,
And Antonio lets the bonds be forfeit.
   BOSOLA.   Strange! (*aside*) This is cunning.
170 DUCHESS.   And hereupon
My brother's bills at Naples are protested
Against. Call up our officers.
   BOSOLA.   I shall.   (*Exit*)

(*Re-enter* ANTONIO)

   DUCHESS.   The place that you must fly to is Ancona:
Hire a house there; I'll send after you
175 My treasure and my jewels. Our weak safety
Runs upon enginous wheels: short syllables
Must stand for periods. I must now accuse you
Of such a feignèd crime as Tasso calls
Magnanima menzogna, a noble lie,

167 engaged with under bond to 168 Ta'en up of lent by
171 protested declared forfeit 176 enginous wheels smooth
running wheels of engines 177 periods sentences

'Cause it must shield our honors. Hark! They are coming.   180

(*Re-enter* BOSOLA *and* OFFICERS)

ANTONIO.   Will Your Grace hear me?
DUCHESS.   I have got well by you; you have yielded
   me
A million of loss: I am like to inherit
The people's curses for your stewardship.
You had the trick in audit-time to be sick,   185
Till I had signed your *quietus;* and that cured you
Without help of a doctor. Gentlemen,
I would have this man be an example to you all;
So shall you hold my favor; I pray, let him;
For h'as done that, alas, you would not think of,   190
And, because I intend to be rid of him,
I mean not to publish. Use your fortune elsewhere.
   ANTONIO.   I am strongly armed to brook my over-
      throw;
As commonly men bear with a hard year,
I will not blame the cause on 't; but do think   195
The necessity of my malevolent star
Procures this, not her humor. Oh, the inconstant
And rotten ground of service! You may see,
'Tis even like him, that in a winter night,
Takes a long slumber o'er a dying fire,   200
A-loth to part from 't; yet parts thence as cold
As when he first sat down.
   DUCHESS.   We do confiscate,
Towards the satisfying of your accounts,
All that you have.
   ANTONIO.   I am all yours, and 'tis very fit
All mine should be so.
   DUCHESS.   So, sir, you have your pass.   205
   ANTONIO.   You may see, gentlemen, what 'tis to serve
A prince with body and soul.   (*Exit*)
   BOSOLA.   Here's an example for extortion: what
moisture is drawn out of the sea, when foul weather
comes, pours down, and runs into the sea again.   210

186 quietus receipt 189 let prevent, with the double meaning "allow"

DUCHESS.   I would know what are your opinions of
this Antonio.

SECOND OFFICER.   He could not abide to see a pig's
head gaping: I thought Your Grace would find him a
215 Jew.

THIRD OFFICER.   I would you had been his officer,
for your own sake.

FOURTH OFFICER.   You would have had more money.

FIRST OFFICER.   He stopped his ears with black
220 wool, and to those came to him for money said he was
thick of hearing.

SECOND OFFICER.   Some said he was an hermaphro-
dite, for he could not abide a woman.

FOURTH OFFICER.   How scurvy proud he would look
225 when the treasury was full ! Well, let him go!

FIRST OFFICER.   Yes, and the chippings of the buttery fly after him, to scour his gold chain!

DUCHESS.   Leave us. [*Exeunt* OFFICERS] What do
you think of these?

230   BOSOLA.   That these are rogues that in 's prosperity,
but to have waited on his fortune, could have wished
his dirty stirrup riveted through their noses, and fol-
lowed after 's mule, like a bear in a ring; would have
prostituted their daughters to his lust; made their first-
235 born intelligencers; thought none happy but such as
were born under his blest planet, and wore his livery:
and do these lice drop off now? Well, never look to
have the like again: he hath left a sort of flattering
rogues behind him; their doom must follow. Princes
240 pay flatterers in their own money: flatterers dissemble
their vices, and they dissemble their lies; that 's justice.
Alas, poor gentleman!

DUCHESS.   Poor? He hath amply filled his coffers.

BOSOLA.   Sure, he was too honest. Pluto, the god
245 of riches, when he 's sent by Jupiter to any man, he
goes limping, to signify that wealth that comes on God's
name comes slowly; but when he 's sent on the devil's
errand, he rides post and comes in by scuttles. Let me

226 **chippings of the buttery** bread crumbs 227 **chain** badge
of the office of a steward 238 **sort** set 248 **scuttles** quick
steps

show you what a most unvalued jewel you have in a
wanton humor thrown away, to bless the man shall   250
find him. He was an excellent courtier and most faith-
ful; a soldier that thought it as beastly to know his own
value too little as devilish to acknowledge it too much.
Both his virtue and form deserved a far better fortune:
his discourse rather delighted to judge itself than show   255
itself: his breast was filled with all perfection, and yet
it seemed a private whispering-room, it made so little
noise of 't.

DUCHESS.   But he was basely descended.

BOSOLA.   Will you make yourself a mercenary her-   260
ald, rather to examine men's pedigrees than virtues?
You shall want him: for know, an honest statesman
to a prince is like a cedar planted by a spring; the
spring bathes the tree's root, the grateful tree rewards
it with his shadow: you have not done so. I would   265
sooner swim to the Bermoothes on two politicians' rotten bladders, tied together with an intelligencer's heart-
string, than depend on so changeable a prince's favor.
Fare thee well, Antonio! Since the malice of the world
would needs down with thee, it cannot be said yet   270
that any ill happened unto thee, considering thy fall
was accompanied with virtue.

DUCHESS.   Oh, you render me excellent music!

BOSOLA.   Say you?

DUCHESS.   This good one that you speak of is my
husband.

BOSOLA.   Do I not dream? Can this ambitious age   275
Have so much goodness in 't as to prefer
A man merely for worth, without these shadows
Of wealth and painted honors? Possible?

DUCHESS.   I have had three children by him.

BOSOLA.   Fortunate lady!
For you have made your private nuptial bed   280
The humble and fair seminary of peace.
No question but many an unbeneficed scholar
Shall pray for you for this deed, and rejoice

249 **unvalued** invaluable 260 **herald** an official whose duty
it was to authenticate pedigrees 266 **Bermoothes** Bermudas
281 **seminary** seedplot

That some preferment in the world can yet
285 Arise from merit. The virgins of your land
That have no dowries shall hope your example
Will raise them to rich husbands. Should you want
Soldiers, 'twould make the very Turks and Moors
Turn Christians, and serve you for this act.
290 Last, the neglected poets of your time,
In honor of this trophy of a man,
Raised by that curious engine, your white hand,
Shall thank you, in your grave, for 't; and make that
More reverend than all the cabinets
295 Of living princes. For Antonio,
His fame shall likewise flow from many a pen,
When heralds shall want coats to sell to men.
    DUCHESS.   As I taste comfort in this friendly speech,
So would I find concealment.
300   BOSOLA.   Oh, the secret of my prince,
Which I will wear on th' inside of my heart!
    DUCHESS.   You shall take charge of all my coin and
       jewels,
And follow him; for he retires himself
To Ancona.
    BOSOLA.   So.
    DUCHESS.   Whither, within few days,
I mean to follow thee.
305   BOSOLA.   Let me think:
I would wish your grace to feign a pilgrimage
To our Lady of Loretto, scarce seven leagues
From fair Ancona; so may you depart
Your country with more honor, and your flight
310 Will seem a princely progress, retaining
Your usual train about you.
    DUCHESS.   Sir, your direction
Shall lead me by the hand.
    CARIOLA.   In my opinion,
She were better progress to the baths at Lucca,
Or go visit the Spa in Germany;
315 For, if you will believe me, I do not like
This jesting with religion, this feigned
Pilgrimage.
    307 Loretto a famous shrine, fifteen miles from Ancona

DUCHESS. Thou art a superstitious fool.
Prepare us instantly for our departure.
Past sorrows, let us moderately lament them;   320
For those to come, seek wisely to prevent them.
           (*Exit* [DUCHESS, *with* CARIOLA.])
  BOSOLA. A politician is the devil's quilted anvil;
He fashions all sins on him, and the blows
Are never heard: he may work in a lady's chamber,
As here for proof. What rests but I reveal   325
All to my lord? Oh, this base quality
Of intelligencer! Why, every quality i' th' world
Prefers but gain or commendation:
Now for this act I am certain to be raised,
And men that paint weeds to the life are praised.   330

SCENE III

    ([*Enter*] CARDINAL, FERDINAND, MALATESTE,
          PESCARA, SILVIO, DELIO)

  CARDINAL. Must we turn soldier, then?
  MALATESTE.   The emperor,
Hearing your worth that way, ere you attained
This reverend garment, joins you in commission
With the right fortunate soldier the Marquis of Pescara,
And the famous Lannoy.
  CARDINAL.   He that had the honor   5
Of taking the French king prisoner?
  MALATESTE.   The same.
Here 's a plot drawn for a new fortification
At Naples.   (*They talk apart*)
  FERDINAND. This great Count Malateste, I perceive,
Hath got employment?
  DELIO.   No employment, my lord;   10
A marginal note in the muster-book, that he is
A voluntary lord.
  FERDINAND. He 's no soldier?

325 **rests** remains 326 **quality** trade 1 **The emperor** Charles
V 4 **Pescara** in actuality, a brother-in-law of Ferdinand 5
Lannoy a favorite general of Charles V's 6 **French king**
Francis I, at Pavia 12 **voluntary lord** a lord who is a volun-
teer

DELIO. He has worn gunpowder in 's hollow tooth
   for the toothache.

15 SILVIO. He comes to the leaguer with a full intent
To eat fresh beef and garlic, means to stay
Till the scent be gone, and straight return to court.

DELIO. He hath read all the late service as the city
chronicle relates it, and keeps two pewterers going,
20 only to express battles in model.

SILVIO. Then he'll fight by the book.

DELIO. By the almanac, I think, to choose good
days and shun the critical. That 's his mistress' scarf

SILVIO. Yes, he protests he would do much for that
25 taffeta.

DELIO. I think he would run away from a battle,
to save it from taking prisoner.

SILVIO. He is horribly afraid gunpowder will spoil
the perfume on 't.

30 DELIO. I saw a Dutchman break his pate once for
calling him pot-gun; he made his head have a bore in
't like a musket.

SILVIO. I would he had made a touchhole to 't. He
is indeed a guarded sumpter-cloth, only for the remove
35 of the court.

(*Enter* BOSOLA *and speaks to* FERDINAND *and the*
CARDINAL)

PESCARA. Bosola arrived? What should be the busi-
ness?
Some falling-out amongst the cardinals.
These factions amongst great men, they are like
Foxes; when their heads are divided,
40 They carry fire in their tails, and all the country
About them goes to wrack for 't.

SILVIO.   What 's that Bosola?

DELIO. I knew him in Padua—a fantastical scholar,
like such who study to know how many knots was in
Hercules' club, of what color Achilles' beard was, or

18 **service** account of military operations 19 **pewterers**
metal-workers 27 **taking** being taken 31 **pot-gun** braggart
34 **sumpter-cloth** horse-cloth 39-40 **Foxes . . . tails** *Judges.*
xv. 11.

whether Hector were not troubled with the toothache. **45**
He hath studied himself half blear-eyed to know the
true symmetry of Caesar's nose by a shoeing-horn; and
this he did to gain the name of a speculative man.

PESCARA.   Mark Prince Ferdinand:
A very salamander lives in 's eye,   **50**
To mock the eager violence of fire.

SILVIO.   That Cardinal hath made more bad faces
with his oppression than ever Michael Angelo made
good ones: he lifts up 's nose, like a foul porpoise
before a storm.   **55**

PESCARA.   The Lord Ferdinand laughs.

DELIO.   Like a deadly cannon that lightens ere it
smokes.

PESCARA.   These are your true pangs of death,
The pangs of life, that struggle with great statesmen.

DELIO.   In such a deformed silence witches whisper **60**
Their charms.

CARDINAL.   Doth she make religion her riding-hood
To keep her from the sun and tempest?

FERDINAND.   That,
That damns her. Methinks her fault and beauty,   *kids get*
Blended together, show like leprosy,   **65**
The whiter, the fouler. I make it a question   *the boot.*
Whether her beggarly brats were ever christened.

CARDINAL.   I will instantly solicit the state of Ancona
To have them banished.

FERDINAND.   You are for Loretto?
I shall not be at your ceremony; fare you well.   **70**
Write to the Duke of Malfi, my young nephew
She had by her first husband, and acquaint him
With 's mother's honesty.

BOSOLA.   I will.

FERDINAND.   Antonio!
A slave that only smelled of ink and counters,
And never in 's life looked like a gentleman,   **75**
But in the audit-time. Go, go presently,
Draw me out an hundred and fifty of our horse,
And meet me at the fort-bridge.   (*Exeunt*)

76 presently at once

SCENE IV

([*Enter*] TWO PILGRIMS *to the Shrine of our
Lady of Loretto*)

FIRST PILGRIM.   I have not seen a goodlier shrine
   than this;
Yet I have visited many.
   SECOND PILGRIM.   The Cardinal of Arragon
Is this day to resign his cardinal's hat:
His sister duchess likewise is arrived
5 To pay her vow of pilgrimage. I expect
A noble ceremony.
   FIRST PILGRIM.   No question. They come.

(*Here the ceremony of the* CARDINAL'S *installment, in
   the habit of a soldier,* [*is*] *performed in delivering
   up his cross, hat, robes, and ring, at the shrine, and
   investing him with sword, helmet, shield, and
   spurs; then* ANTONIO, *the* DUCHESS, *and their children, having presented themselves at the shrine,
   are, by a form of banishment in dumb-show expressed towards them by the* CARDINAL *and the
   state of Ancona, banished: during all which ceremony, this ditty is sung, to very solemn music, by
   divers churchmen*)

Arms and honors deck thy story,
To thy fame's eternal glory!
10 Adverse fortune ever fly thee;
No disastrous fate come nigh thee!

I alone will sing thy praises,
Whom to honor virtue raises;
And thy study, that divine is,
15 Bent to martial discipline is.

8-23 In the quarto of 1623, Webster disclaims the author-
ship of this song.

Lay aside all those robes lie by thee;
Crown thy arts with arms, they'll beautify thee.

O worthy of worthiest name, adorned in this manner,
Lead bravely thy forces on under war's warlike banner!
Oh, mayst thou prove fortunate in all martial courses! 20
Guide thou still by skill in arts and forces!
Victory attend thee nigh, whilst fame sings loud thy
    powers;
Triumphant conquest crown thy head, and blessings
    pour down showers!
                (*Exeunt all except the* TWO PILGRIMS)
  FIRST PILGRIM.   Here 's a strange turn of state! Who
    would have thought
So great a lady would have matched herself   25
Unto so mean a person? Yet the Cardinal
Bears himself much too cruel.
  SECOND PILGRIM.   They are banished.
  FIRST PILGRIM. But I would ask what power hath
    this state
Of Ancona to determine of a free prince.
  SECOND PILGRIM. They are a free state, sir, and her
    brother showed   30
How that the Pope, fore-hearing of her looseness,
Hath seized into th' protection of the Church
The dukedom which she held as dowager.
  FIRST PILGRIM. But by what justice?
  SECOND PILGRIM.   Sure, I think by none,
Only her brother's instigation.   35
  FIRST PILGRIM. What was it with such violence he
    took
Off from her finger?
  SECOND PILGRIM.   'Twas her wedding-ring,
Which he vowed shortly he would sacrifice
To his revenge.
  FIRST PILGRIM. Alas, Antonio!
If that a man be thrust into a well,   40
No matter who sets hands to 't, his own weight
Will bring him sooner to th' bottom. Come, let 's hence.
Fortune makes this conclusion general,
All things do help th' unhappy man to fall. (*Exeunt*)

Scene V

([*Enter*] Duchess, Antonio, *Children*, Cariola,
and Servants)

Duchess.   Banished Ancona?

Antonio.   Yes, you see what power
Lightens in great men's breath.

Duchess.   Is all our train
Shrunk to this poor remainder?

Antonio.   These poor men,
Which have got little in your service, vow
5 To take your fortune, but your wiser buntings,
Now they are fledged, are gone.

Duchess.   They have done wisely.
This puts me in mind of death: physicians thus,
With their hands full of money, use to give o'er
Their patients.

Antonio.   Right the fashion of the world:
10 From decayed fortunes every flatterer shrinks;
Men cease to build where the foundation sinks.

Duchess.   I had a very strange dream to-night.

Antonio.   What was 't?

Duchess.   Methought I wore my coronet of state,
And on a sudden all the diamonds
Were changed to pearls.

15 Antonio.   My interpretation
Is, you'll weep shortly, for to me the pearls
Do signify your tears.

Duchess.   The birds that live
I' th' field on the wild benefit of nature
Live happier than we; for they may choose their mates,
20 And carol their sweet pleasures to the spring.

(*Enter* Bosola *with a letter*)

Bosola.   You are happily o'erta'en.

Duchess.   From my brother?

Bosola.   Yes, from the Lord Ferdinand your brother
All love and safety.

5 take share in 8 use are accustomed to 9 Right the Exactly
the 12 to-night last night

Ferd, trying to be sneaky

DUCHESS.   Thou dost blanch mischief,
Wouldst make it white. See, see, like to calm weather
At sea before a tempest, false hearts speak fair   25
To those they intend most mischief.
"Send Antonio to me; I want his head in a business."
A politic equivocation!
He doth not want your counsel, but your head;
That is, he cannot sleep till you be dead.   30
And here 's another pitfall that 's strewed o'er
With roses: mark it, 'tis a cunning one:
"I stand engaged for your husband for several debts at
Naples: let not that trouble him; I had rather have his
heart than his money."   35
And I believe so too.
    BOSOLA.   What do you believe?
    DUCHESS.   That he so much distrusts my husband's
        love,
He will by no means believe his heart is with him
Until he see it: the devil is not cunning
Enough to circumvent us in riddles.   40
    BOSOLA.   Will you reject that noble and free league
Of amity and love which I present you?
    DUCHESS.   Their league is like that of some politic
        kings,
Only to make themselves of strength and power
To be our after-ruin: tell them so.   45
    BOSOLA.   And what from you?
    ANTONIO.   Thus tell him: I will not come.
    BOSOLA.   And what of this? (*Pointing to the letter*)
    ANTONIO.   My brothers have dispersed
Blood-hounds abroad; which till I hear are muzzled,
No truce, though hatched with ne'er such politic skill,
Is safe, that hangs upon our enemies' will.   50
I'll not come at them.
    BOSOLA.   This proclaims your breeding:
Every small thing draws a base mind to fear,
As the adamant draws iron. Fare you well, sir;
You shall shortly hear from 's.   (*Exit*)
    DUCHESS.   I suspect some ambush;
Therefore, by all my love I do conjure you   55
23 **blanch** bleach

To take your eldest son, and fly towards Milan.
Let us not venture all this poor remainder
In one unlucky bottom.

    ANTONIO.   You counsel safely.
Best of my life, farewell. Since we must part,
60 Heaven hath a hand in 't, but no otherwise
Than as some curious artist takes in sunder
A clock or watch, when it is out of frame,
To bring 't in better order.

    DUCHESS.   I know not
Which is best, to see you dead, or part with you.
65 Farewell, boy.
Thou art happy that thou hast not understanding
To know thy misery; for all our wit
And reading brings us to a truer sense
Of sorrow. In the eternal church, sir,
I do hope we shall not part thus.

70   ANTONIO.   Oh, be of comfort!
Make patience a noble fortitude,
And think not how unkindly we are used:
Man, like to cassia, is proved best being bruised.

    DUCHESS.   Must I, like to a slave-born Russian,
75 Account it praise to suffer tyranny?
And yet, O heaven, thy heavy hand is in 't!
I have seen my little boy oft scourge his top,
And compared myself to 't: naught made me e'er
Go right but heaven's scourge-stick.

    ANTONIO.   Do not weep;
80 Heaven fashioned us of nothing, and we strive
To bring ourselves to nothing. Farewell, Cariola,
And thy sweet armful. If I do never see thee more,
Be a good mother to your little ones,
And save them from the tiger. Fare you well.

    DUCHESS.   Let me look upon you once more, for
85   that speech
Came from a dying father. Your kiss is colder
Than that I have seen an holy anchorite
Give to a dead man's skull.

58 **bottom** ship   62 **frame** order   73 **cassia** cinnamon   74-75
Must I . . . tyranny idea and phrasing from Sidney's *Astrophel and Stella*

ANTONIO.   My heart is turned to a heavy lump of
  lead,
With which I sound my danger. Fare you well.   90
                    (*Exeunt* ANTONIO *and his Son*)
  DUCHESS.   My laurel is all withered.
  CARIOLA.   Look, madam, what a troop of armèd
  men
Make toward us.
  DUCHESS.   Oh, they are very welcome:
When Fortune's wheel is over-charged with princes,
The weight makes it move swift: I would have my ruin 95
Be sudden.

     (*Enter* BOSOLA [*vizarded,*] *with a Guard*)

                    I am your adventure, am I not?
  BOSOLA.   You are. You must see your husband no
  more.
  DUCHESS.   What devil art thou that counterfeits
  heaven's thunder?
  BOSOLA.   Is that terrible? I would have you tell me
  whether
Is that note worse that frights the silly birds   100
Out of the corn, or that which doth allure them
To the nets? You have hearkened to the last too much.
  DUCHESS.   Oh, misery! Like to a rusty o'ercharged
  cannon,
Shall I never fly in pieces? Come, to what prison?
  BOSOLA.   To none.
  DUCHESS.   Whither, then?
  BOSOLA.   To your palace.
  DUCHESS.   I have heard 105
That Charon's boat serves to convey all o'er
The dismal lake, but brings none back again.
  BOSOLA.   Your brothers mean you safety and pity.
  DUCHESS.   Pity!
With such a pity men preserve alive
Pheasants and quails, when they are not fat enough   110
To be eaten.
  BOSOLA.   These are your children?

106 **Charon** the boatman of the River Styx 109-111 **With
such a pity . . . eaten** idea from Sidney's *Arcadia*

DUCHESS.   Yes.
BOSOLA.   Can they prattle?
DUCHESS.   No.
But I intend, since they were born accursed,
Curses shall be their first language.
    BOSOLA.   Fie, madam!
Forget this base, low fellow—
115   DUCHESS.   Were I a man,
I'd beat that counterfeit face into thy other.
    BOSOLA.   One of no birth.
    DUCHESS.   Say that he was born mean,
Man is most happy when 's own actions
Be arguments and examples of his virtue.
120   BOSOLA.   A barren, beggarly virtue!
    DUCHESS.   I prithee, who is greatest? Can you tell?
Sad tales befit my woe: I'll tell you one.
A salmon, as she swam unto the sea,
Met with a dog-fish, who encounters her
125 With this rough language: "Why art thou so bold
To mix thyself with our high state of floods,
Being no eminent courtier, but one
That for the calmest and fresh time o' the year
Dost live in shallow rivers, rank'st thyself
130 With silly smelts and shrimps? And darest thou
Pass by our dog-ship without reverence?"
"Oh!" quoth the salmon, "sister, be at peace:
Thank Jupiter we both have passed the net!
Our value never can be truly known,
135 Till in the fisher's basket we be shown:
I' th' market then my price may be the higher,
Even when I am nearest to the cook and fire."
So to great men the moral may be stretchèd;
Men oft are valued high, when they're most wretched.
140 But come, whither you please. I am armed 'gainst
    misery;
Bent to all sways of the oppressor's will:
There 's no deep valley but near some great hill.
                         (Ex[eunt])

116 counterfeit face mask

Act IV

❀

Scene I

(*Enter* FERDINAND *and* BOSOLA)

FERDINAND.   How doth our sister duchess bear her-
self
In her imprisonment?
　　BOSOLA.　　　　　Nobly. I'll describe her.
She 's sad as one long used to 't, and she seems
Rather to welcome the end of misery
Than shun it; a behavior so noble   5
As gives a majesty to adversity:
You may discern the shape of loveliness
More perfect in her tears than in her smiles;
She will muse four hours together; and her silence,
Methinks, expresseth more than if she spake.   10
　　FERDINAND.   Her melancholy seems to be fortified
With a strange disdain.
　　BOSOLA.　　　　　'Tis so; and this restraint,
Like English mastiffs that grow fierce with tying,
Makes her too passionately apprehend
Those pleasures she 's kept from.
　　FERDINAND.　　　　　Curse upon her!   15
I will no longer study in the book
Of another's heart. Inform her what I told you. (*Exit*)

(*Enter* DUCHESS *and Attendants*)

BOSOLA.   All comfort to your grace!
　　DUCHESS.　　　　　　I will have none.
Pray thee, why dost thou wrap thy poisoned pills
In gold and sugar?   20

3-6 **She's sad . . . adversity** idea and phrasing from Sidney's *Arcadia*

63

BOSOLA.   Your elder brother, the Lord Ferdinand,
Is come to visit you, and sends you word,
'Cause once he rashly made a solemn vow
Never to see you more, he comes i' th' night,
25 And prays you gently neither torch nor taper
Shine in your chamber. He will kiss your hand
And reconcile himself, but for his vow
He dares not see you.
    DUCHESS.   At his pleasure. Take hence
      the lights.
He 's come.

(*Enter* FERDINAND)

    FERDINAND.   Where are you?
    DUCHESS.   Here, sir.
30   FERDINAND.   This darkness suits you well.
    DUCHESS.   I would ask you pardon.
    FERDINAND.   You have it, for I account it
The honorabl'st revenge, where I may kill,
To pardon. Where are your cubs?
    DUCHESS.   Whom?
    FERDINAND.   Call them your children;
For though our national law distinguish bastards
35 From true legitimate issue, compassionate nature
Makes them all equal.
    DUCHESS.   Do you visit me for this?
You violate a sacrament o' th' Church
Shall make you howl in hell for 't.
    FERDINAND.   It had been well
Could you have lived thus always; for, indeed,
40 You were too much i' th' light—but no more—
I come to seal my peace with you. Here 's a hand
                (*Gives her a dead man's hand*)
To which you have vowed much love; the ring upon 't
You gave.
    DUCHESS.   I affectionately kiss it.
    FERDINAND.   Pray, do, and bury the print of it in
      your heart.
45 I will leave this ring with you for a love-token,

41 hand The devices of the dead man's hand and the waxen
corpses are adapted from incidents in Sidney's *Arcadia*

And the hand as sure as the ring, and do not doubt
But you shall have the heart, too. When you need a
 friend,
Send it to him that owed it; you shall see
Whether he can aid you.
 Duchess.   You are very cold;
I fear you are not well after your travel.   **50**
Ha! Lights! Oh, horrible!
 Ferdinand. Let her have lights enough. (*Exit*)
 Duchess. What witchcraft doth he practise, that
 he hath left
A dead man's hand here?

(*Here is discovered, behind a traverse, the artificial
figures of Antonio and his Children, appearing as
if they were dead*)

 Bosola. Look you, here 's the piece from which
 'twas ta'en.
He doth present you this sad spectacle,   **55**
That, now you know directly they are dead,
Hereafter you may wisely cease to grieve
For that which cannot be recovered.
 Duchess. There is not between heaven and earth
 one wish
I stay for after this: it wastes me more   **60**
Than were 't my picture, fashioned out of wax,
Stuck with a magical needle, and then buried
In some foul dunghill; and yond 's an excellent property
For a tyrant, which I would account mercy.
 Bosola.   What 's that?
 Duchess. If they would bind me to that lifeless
 trunk   **65**
And let me freeze to death.
 Bosola.   Come, you must live.
 Duchess. That 's the greatest torture souls feel in
 hell,
In hell, that they must live, and cannot die.

---

48 owed owned **61-63 picture . . . dunghill** a traditional
practice of witches, to destroy an enemy

Portia, I'll new-kindle thy coals again,

70 And revive the rare and almost dead example
Of a loving wife.

BOSOLA.   Oh, fie! Despair? Remember
You are a Christian.

DUCHESS.   The Church enjoins fasting:
I'll starve myself to death.

BOSOLA.   Leave this vain sorrow.
Things being at the worst begin to mend: the bee

75 When he hath shot his sting into your hand, may then
Play with your eyelid.

DUCHESS.   Good comfortable fellow,
Persuade a wretch that 's broke upon the wheel
To have all his bones new set; entreat him live
To be executed again. Who must dispatch me?

80 I account this world a tedious theatre,
For I do play a part in 't 'gainst my will.

BOSOLA.   Come, be of comfort; I will save your life.

DUCHESS.   Indeed,
I have not leisure to tend so small a business.

BOSOLA.   Now, by my life, I pity you.

DUCHESS.   Thou art a fool, then,

85 To waste thy pity on a thing so wretched
As cannot pity it[self]. I am full of daggers.
Puff, let me blow these vipers from me.

(*Enter* SERVANT)

What are you?

SERVANT.   One that wishes you long life.

DUCHESS.   I would thou wert hanged for the horrible curse

90 Thou hast given me. I shall shortly grow one
Of the miracles of pity. I'll go pray—
No, I'll go curse.

BOSOLA.   Oh, fie!

DUCHESS.   I could curse the stars—

BOSOLA.   Oh, fearful!

69 **Portia** the devoted wife of Brutus, who committed sui-
cide by swallowing hot coals 88-90 This situation and the
Duchess' retort are borrowed from Sidney's *Arcadia*

DUCHESS.   And those three smiling seasons of the
  year
Into a Russian winter, nay, the world   95
To its first chaos.
  BOSOLA.   Look you, the stars shine still.
  DUCHESS.   Oh, but you must
Remember, my curse hath a great way to go.
Plagues, that make lanes through largest families,
Consume them!   100
  BOSOLA.   Fie, lady!
  DUCHESS.   Let them, like tyrants,
Never be remembered but for the ill they have done;
Let all the zealous prayers of mortified
Churchmen forget them!
  BOSOLA.   Oh, uncharitable!
  DUCHESS.   Let Heaven a little while cease crowning
    martyrs   105
To punish them!
Go, howl them this, and say, I long to bleed:
It is some mercy when men kill with speed.
                  (*Exeunt* DUCHESS *and Attendants*)

            (*Re-enter* FERDINAND)

  FERDINAND.   Excellent, as I would wish; she 's
    plagued in art:
These presentations are but framed in wax   110
By the curious master in that quality,
Vincentio Lauriola, and she takes them
For true substantial bodies.
  BOSOLA.   Why do you do this?
  FERDINAND.   To bring her to despair.
  BOSOLA.   'Faith, end here,
And go no farther in your cruelty.   115
Send her a penitential garment to put on
Next to her delicate skin, and furnish her
With beads and prayer-books.
  FERDINAND.   Damn her! That body of hers,
While that my blood ran pure in 't, was more worth
Than that which thou wouldst comfort, called a soul. 120
I will send her masks of common courtezans,

111 quality profession

Have her meat served up by bawds and ruffians,
And, 'cause she'll needs be mad, I am resolved
To remove forth the common hospital
125 All the mad-folk, and place them near her lodging;
There let them practise together, sing and dance,
And act their gambols to the full o' th' moon:
If she can sleep the better for it, let her.
Your work is almost ended.

BOSOLA.   Must I see her again?
FERDINAND.   Yes.
BOSOLA.   Never.
130 FERDINAND.   You must.
BOSOLA.   Never in mine own shape;
That 's forfeited by my intelligence
And this last cruel lie. When you send me next,
The business shall be comfort.
FERDINAND.   Very likely.
135 Thy pity is nothing of kin to thee. Antonio
Lurks about Milan: thou shalt shortly thither
To feed a fire as great as my revenge,
Which ne'er will slack till it have spent his fuel.
Intemperate agues make physicians cruel.   (*Exeunt*)

SCENE II

(*Enter* DUCHESS *and* CARIOLA)

DUCHESS.   What hideous noise was that?
CARIOLA.   'Tis the wild consort
Of madmen, lady, which your tyrant brother
Hath placed about your lodging. This tyranny,
I think, was never practised till this hour.
DUCHESS.   Indeed, I thank him. Nothing but noise
5   and folly
Can keep me in my right wits, whereas reason
And silence make me stark mad. Sit down;
Discourse to me some dismal tragedy.
CARIOLA.   Oh, 'twill increase your melancholy.
DUCHESS.   Thou art deceived:
10 To hear of greater grief would lessen mine.

132 intelligence conduct as a paid informer 138 his fuel its
fuel 1 consort company

This is a prison?

    CARIOLA.   Yes, but you shall live
To shake this durance off.

    DUCHESS.   Thou art a fool:
The robin-redbreast and the nightingale
Never live long in cages.

    CARIOLA.   Pray, dry your eyes.
What think you of, madam?

    DUCHESS.   Of nothing; when I muse thus, 15
I sleep.

    CARIOLA.   Like a madman, with your eyes open?

    DUCHESS.   Dost thou think we shall know one an-
    other in th' other world?

    CARIOLA.   Yes, out of question.

    DUCHESS.   Oh, that it were possible
We might but hold some two days' conference
With the dead! From them I should learn somewhat,
    I am sure,   20
I never shall know here. I'll tell thee a miracle;
I am not mad yet, to my cause of sorrow:
Th' heaven o'er my head seems made of molten brass,
The earth of flaming sulphur, yet I am not mad.
I am acquainted with sad misery   25
As the tanned galley-slave is with his oar;
Necessity makes me suffer constantly,
And custom makes it easy. Who do I look like now?

    CARIOLA.   Like to your picture in the gallery,
A deal of life in show, but none in practice,   30
Or rather like some reverend monument
Whose ruins are even pitied.

    DUCHESS.   Very proper.
And Fortune seems only to have her eyesight
To behold my tragedy.
How now! What noise is that?

              (*Enter* SERVANT)

    SERVANT.   I am come to tell you 35
Your brother hath intended you some sport.

13-14 **The robin-redbreast . . . cages** idea borrowed from
Tofte's translation of Ariosto's *Satires* 29-30 **picture . . .
practice** phrasing from Sidney's *Arcadia*

A great physician, when the Pope was sick
Of a deep melancholy, presented him
With several sorts of madmen, which wild object
40 Being full of change and sport, forced him to laugh,
And so the imposthume broke. The self-same cure
The duke intends on you.

DUCHESS.   Let them come in.

SERVANT.   There 's a mad lawyer; and a secular
     priest;
A doctor that hath forfeited his wits
45 By jealousy; an astrologian
That in his works said such a day o' th' month
Should be the day of doom, and, failing of 't,
Ran mad; an English tailor crazed i' th' brain
With the study of new fashions; a gentleman-usher
50 Quite beside himself with care to keep in mind
The number of his lady's salutations
Or 'How do you['s]' she employed him in each morning;
A farmer, too, an excellent knave in grain,
Mad 'cause he was hindered transportation:
55 And let one broker that 's mad loose to these,
You'd think the devil were among them.

DUCHESS.   Sit, Cariola. Let them loose when you
     please,
For I am chained to endure all your tyranny.

(*Enter* MADMEN)

(*Here by a* MADMAN *this Song is sung to a dismal kind of music*)

Oh, let us howl some heavy note,
60   Some deadly dogged howl,
     Sounding as from the threatening throat
          Of beasts and fatal fowl!
     As ravens, screech-owls, bulls, and bears,
          We'll bell, and bawl our parts,
65   Till irksome noise have cloyed your ears
          And corrosived your hearts.
     At last, whenas our quire wants breath,

39 **sorts** groups 41 **imposthume** abscess 53 **in grain** pun on
ingrained and in the grain trade

         Our bodies being blest,
      We'll sing, like swans, to welcome death,
         And die in love and rest.   **70**

FIRST MADMAN.   Doom's-day not come yet? I'll draw
it nearer by a perspective, or make a glass that shall
set all the world on fire upon an instant. I cannot sleep;
my pillow is stuffed with a litter of porcupines.

SECOND MADMAN.   Hell is a mere glass-house, where **75**
the devils are continually blowing up women's souls
on hollow irons, and the fire never goes out.

THIRD MADMAN. I will lie with every woman in
my parish the tenth night; I will tithe them over like
haycocks.   **80**

FOURTH MADMAN.   Shall my pothecary out-go me
because I am a cuckold? I have found out his roguery;
he makes alum of his wife's urine, and sells it to Puritans that have sore throats with overstraining.

FIRST MADMAN.   I have skill in heraldry.   **85**

SECOND MADMAN.   Hast?

FIRST MADMAN. You do give for your crest a wood-
cock's head with the brains picked out on 't; you are
a very ancient gentleman.

THIRD MADMAN.   Greek is turned Turk: we are only **90**
to be saved by the Helvetian translation.

FIRST MADMAN.   Come on, sir, I will lay the law
to you.

SECOND MADMAN.   Oh, rather lay a corrosive: the
law will eat to the bone.   **95**

THIRD MADMAN.   He that drinks but to satisfy nature is damned.

FOURTH MADMAN.   If I had my glass here, I would
show a sight should make all the women here call me
mad doctor.   **100**

FIRST MADMAN.   What's he? A rope-maker?

SECOND MADMAN.   No, no, no, a snuffling knave
that, while he shows the tombs, will have his hand in
a wench's placket.

THIRD MADMAN.   Woe to the caroche that brought **105**

72 **perspective** telescope   84 **overstraining** from psalm-singing
91 **Helvetian translation** the Calvinist translation popular
with Puritans   105 **caroche** coach

home my wife from the masque at three o'clock in the
morning! It had a large feather-bed in it.

FOURTH MADMAN. I have pared the devil's nails
forty times, roasted them in raven's eggs, and cured
110 agues with them.

THIRD MADMAN. Get me three hundred milchbats,
to make possets to procure sleep.

FOURTH MADMAN. All the college may throw their
caps at me: I have made a soap-boiler costive; it was
115 my masterpiece.

(*Here the dance, consisting of* 8 MADMEN, *with
music answerable thereunto; after which*
BOSOLA, *like an old man, enters*)

DUCHESS. Is he mad too?
SERVANT.   Pray, question him. I'll leave you.
                                (*Exeunt* SERVANT *and* MADMEN)
BOSOLA. I am come to make thy tomb.
DUCHESS.   Ha! My tomb?
Thou speak'st as if I lay upon my death-bed,
Gasping for breath. Dost thou perceive me sick?
BOSOLA. Yes, and the more dangerously, since thy
120   sickness
Is insensible.
DUCHESS. Thou art not mad, sure. Dost know me?
BOSOLA. Yes.
DUCHESS.   Who am I?
BOSOLA. Thou art a box of worm-seed, at best but
125 a salvatory of green mummy. What's this flesh? A little
crudded milk, fantastical puff-paste. Our bodies are
weaker than those paper-prisons boys use to keep flies
in, more contemptible, since ours is to preserve earth-
worms. Didst thou ever see a lark in a cage? Such is
130 the soul in the body: this world is like her little turf
of grass, and the heaven o'er our heads, like her look-
ing-glass, only gives us a miserable knowledge of the
small compass of our prison.

112 **possets** hot milk and liquor 113 **throw their caps** do
their utmost 125 **salvatory** ointment-box **green mummy**
undried mummy in use as a drug 126 **crudded** curdled

DUCHESS.   Am not I thy duchess?

BOSOLA.   Thou art some great woman, sure, for riot 135
begins to sit on thy forehead, clad in grey hairs,
twenty years sooner than on a merry milkmaid's. Thou
sleep'st worse than if a mouse should be forced to take
up her lodging in a cat's ear: a little infant that breeds
its teeth, should it lie with thee, would cry out, as if 140
thou wert the more unquiet bed-fellow.   *— can't take away
my identity.*

DUCHESS.   I am Duchess of Malfi still.

BOSOLA.   That makes thy sleeps so broken:
Glories, like glow-worms, afar off shine bright,
But, looked to near, have neither heat nor light.   145

DUCHESS.   Thou art very plain.

BOSOLA.   My trade is to flatter the dead, not the
living; I am a tomb-maker.

DUCHESS.   And thou com'st to make my tomb?

BOSOLA.   Yes.   150

DUCHESS.   Let me be a little merry. Of what stuff
wilt thou make it?

BOSOLA.   Nay, resolve me first, of what fashion?

DUCHESS.   Why, do we grow fantastical in our death-
bed? Do we affect fashion in the grave?   155

BOSOLA.   Most ambitiously. Princes' images on their
tombs do not lie, as they were wont, seeming to pray
up to heaven, but with their hands under their cheeks,
as if they died of the toothache. They are not carved
with their eyes fixed upon the stars, but as their minds 160
were wholly bent upon the world, the self-same way
they seem to turn their faces.

DUCHESS.   Let me know fully therefore the effect
Of this thy dismal preparation,
This talk fit for a charnel.

BOSOLA.   Now I shall.   165

(*[Enter* EXECUTIONERS, *with*] *a coffin, cords, and a bell*)

Here is a present from your princely brothers;
And may it arrive welcome, for it brings
Last benefit, last sorrow.

146 **plain** outspoken 156-162 **Princes' images . . . faces**
This change in the style of tombs came in the sixteenth
century

DUCHESS.   Let me see it:
I have so much obedience in my blood,
170 I wish it in their veins to do them good.
     BOSOLA.   This is your last presence-chamber.
     CARIOLA.   O my sweet lady!
     DUCHESS. Peace; it affrights not me.
     BOSOLA.   I am the common bellman,
That usually is sent to condemned persons
The night before they suffer.
     DUCHESS.   Even now
Thou said'st thou wast a tomb-maker.
175 BOSOLA.   'Twas to bring you
By degrees to mortification. Listen.

          Hark, now every thing is still
          The screech-owl and the whistler shrill
          Call upon our dame aloud,
180   And bid her quickly don her shroud!
          Much you had of land and rent:
          Your length in clay's now competent:
          A long war disturbed your mind;
          Here your perfect peace is signed.
185   Of what is 't fools make such vain keeping?
          Sin their conception, their birth weeping,
          Their life a general mist of error,
          Their death a hideous storm of terror.
          Strew your hair with powders sweet,
190   Don clean linen, bathe your feet,
          And (the foul fiend more to check)
          A crucifix let bless your neck:
          'Tis now full tide 'tween night and day;
          End your groan, and come away.

195 CARIOLA. Hence, villains, tyrants, murderers! Alas!
     What will you do with my lady? Call for help.
        DUCHESS. To whom? To our next neighbors? They
     are madfolks.
        BOSOLA. Remove that noise.

176 mortification a grim pun on penitential discipline and
the coming of death 177 Hark This song was probably sung
by Bosola's attendants 178 whistler a mysterious bird whose
song warned the hearer of impending death

DUCHESS.   Farewell, Cariola.
In my last will I have not much to give:
A many hungry guests have fed upon me;   200
Thine will be a poor reversion.
   CARIOLA.   I will die with her.
   DUCHESS.   I pray thee, look thou giv'st my little boy
Some syrup for his cold, and let the girl
Say her prayers ere she sleep.
      (CARIOLA *is forced out by the* EXECUTIONERS)
                          Now what you please.

What death?
   BOSOLA.   Strangling;   205
Here are your executioners.
   DUCHESS.   I forgive them:
The apoplexy, catarrh, or cough o' th' lungs,
Would do as much as they do.
   BOSOLA.   Doth not death fright you?
   DUCHESS.   Who would be afraid on 't,
Knowing to meet such excellent company   210
In th' other world?
   BOSOLA.   Yet, methinks,
The manner of your death should much afflict you:
This cord should terrify you.
   DUCHESS.   Not a whit.
What would it pleasure me to have my throat cut
With diamonds? Or to be smothered   215
With cassia? Or to be shot to death with pearls?
I know death hath ten thousand several doors
For men to take their exits, and 'tis found
They go on such strange geometrical hinges,
You may open them both ways. Any way, for heaven
   sake,   220
So I were out of your whispering. Tell my brothers
That I perceive death, now I am well awake,
Best gift is they can give or I can take.
I would fain put off my last woman's fault,
I'd not be tedious to you.
   EXECUTIONER.   We are ready.   225
   DUCHESS.   Dispose my breath how please you, but
   my body

216 cassia cinnamon 224 **fault** talkativeness

Bestow upon my women, will you?

EXECUTIONER.   Yes.

DUCHESS.   Pull, and pull strongly, for your able
strength

Must pull down heaven upon me—

230 Yet stay; heaven-gates are not so highly arched
As princes' palaces; they that enter there
Must go upon their knees (*Kneels*). Come, violent
death.

Serve for mandragora to make me sleep!

Go tell my brothers, when I am laid out,

235 They then may feed in quiet.   (*They strangle her*)

BOSOLA.   Where's the waiting woman? Fetch her:
some other

Strangle the children.

            (*Exeunt* EXECUTIONERS, *some of whom return
                                with* CARIOLA)

Look you, there sleeps your mistress.

CARIOLA.   Oh, you are damned
Perpetually for this! My turn is next.

Is 't not so ordered?

240 BOSOLA.   Yes, and I am glad
You are so well prepared for 't.

CARIOLA.   You are deceived, Sir,
I am not prepared for 't, I will not die;
I will first come to my answer, and know
How I have offended.

BOSOLA.   Come, dispatch her.

245 You kept her counsel; now you shall keep ours.

CARIOLA.   I will not die, I must not; I am contracted
To a young gentleman.

EXECUTIONER.   Here's your wedding-ring.

CARIOLA.   Let me but speak with the duke; I'll discover

Treason to his person.

BOSOLA.   Delays! Throttle her.

EXECUTIONER.   She bites and scratches.

250 CARIOLA.   If you kill me now,
I am damned; I have not been at confession
This two years.

233 mandragora drug inducing sleep   243 answer trial

BOSOLA. When!
CARIOLA. I am quick with child.
BOSOLA. Why, then,
Your credit's saved. (*They strangle* CARIOLA)
Bear her into th' next room;
Let this lie still.

(*Exeunt the* EXECUTIONERS *with the body
of* CARIOLA)

(*Enter* FERDINAND)

FERDINAND. Is she dead?
BOSOLA. She is what 255
You'd have her. But here begin your pity.
(*Shows the Children strangled*)
Alas, how have these offended?
FERDINAND. The death
Of young wolves is never to be pitied.
BOSOLA. Fix
Your eye here.
FERDINAND. Constantly.
BOSOLA. Do you not weep?
Other sins only speak; murder shrieks out: 260
The element of water moistens the earth,
But blood flies upwards and bedews the heavens.
FERDINAND. Cover her face; mine eyes dazzle: she
died young.
BOSOLA. I think not so; her infelicity
Seemed to have years too many.
FERDINAND. She and I were twins; 265
And should I die this instant, I had lived
Her time to a minute.
BOSOLA. It seems she was born first:
You have bloodily approved the ancient truth,
That kindred commonly do worse agree
Than remote strangers.
FERDINAND. Let me see her face 270
Again. Why didst not thou pity her? What
An excellent honest man mightst thou have been,
If thou hadst borne her to some sanctuary!
Or, bold in a good cause, opposed thyself,
With thy advancèd sword above thy head, 275

Between her innocence and my revenge!
I bade thee, when I was distracted of my wits,
Go kill my dearest friend, and thou hast done 't.
For let me but examine well the cause:
280 What was the meanness of her match to me?
Only I must confess I had a hope,
Had she continued widow, to have gained
An infinite mass of treasure by her death:
And that was the main cause, her marriage,
285 That drew a stream of gall quite through my heart.
For thee, as we observe in tragedies
That a good actor many times is cursed
For playing a villain's part, I hate thee for 't,
And, for my sake, say thou hast done much ill well.

    BOSOLA. Let me quicken your memory, for I per-
290   ceive
You are falling into ingratitude: I challenge
The reward due to my service.

    FERDINAND.   I'll tell thee
What I'll give thee.

    BOSOLA.   Do.

    FERDINAND.   I'll give thee a pardon
For this murder.

    BOSOLA.   Ha!

    FERDINAND.   Yes, and 'tis
295 The largest bounty I can study to do thee.
By what authority didst thou execute
This bloody sentence?

    BOSOLA.   By yours.

    FERDINAND.   Mine? Was I her judge?
Did any ceremonial form of law
Doom her to not-being? Did a complete jury
300 Deliver her conviction up i' th' court?
Where shalt thou find this judgment registered,
Unless in hell? See, like a bloody fool,
Thou'st forfeited thy life, and thou shalt die for 't.

    BOSOLA.   The office of justice is perverted quite
305 When one thief hangs another. Who shall dare
To reveal this?

    FERDINAND. Oh, I'll tell thee;
The wolf shall find her grave, and scrape it up,

Not to devour the corpse, but to discover
The horrid murder.
    BOSOLA.   You, not I, shall quake for 't.
    FERDINAND. Leave me.
    BOSOLA.   I will first receive my pen-
    sion.   310
    FERDINAND. You are a villain.
    BOSOLA.   When your ingratitude
Is judge, I am so.
    FERDINAND.   Oh, horror, that not the fear
Of Him which binds the devils can prescribe man
Obedience! Never look upon me more.
    BOSOLA.   Why, fare thee well.   315
Your brother and yourself are worthy men:
You have a pair of hearts are hollow graves,
Rotten, and rotting others; and your vengeance,
Like two chained bullets, still goes arm in arm.
You may be brothers, for treason, like the plague,   320
Doth take much in a blood. I stand like one
That long hath ta'en a sweet and golden dream.
I am angry with myself, now that I wake.
    FERDINAND.   Get thee into some unknown part o' th'
    world,
That I may never see thee.
    BOSOLA.   Let me know   325
Wherefore I should be thus neglected. Sir,
I served your tyranny, and rather strove
To satisfy yourself than all the world,
And though I loathed the evil, yet I loved
You that did counsel it; and rather sought   330
To appear a true servant than an honest man.
    FERDINAND.   I'll go hunt the badger by owl-light:
'Tis a deed of darkness.   (*Exit*)
    BOSOLA.   He's much distracted. Off, my painted
    honor!
While with vain hopes our faculties we tire,   335
We seem to sweat in ice and freeze in fire.
What would I do, were this to do again?
I would not change my peace of conscience

321 **take much in a blood** run in families

For all the wealth of Europe. She stirs; here's life.
340 Return, fair soul, from darkness, and lead mine
Out of this sensible hell. She's warm, she breathes.
Upon thy pale lips I will melt my heart,
To store them with fresh color. Who's there!
Some cordial drink! Alas! I dare not call:
345 So pity would destroy pity. Her eye opes,
And heaven in it seems to ope, that late was shut,
To take me up to mercy.
   DUCHESS. Antonio!
   BOSOLA.   Yes, madam, he is living;
The dead bodies you saw were but feigned statues:
350 He's reconciled to your brothers: the Pope hath wrought
The atonement.
   DUCHESS. Mercy!   (*She dies*)
   BOSOLA. Oh, she's gone again! There the cords of
   life broke.
Oh, sacred innocence, that sweetly sleeps
On turtles' feathers, whilst a guilty conscience
355 Is a black register wherein is writ
All our good deeds and bad, a perspective
That shows us hell! That we cannot be suffered
To do good when we have a mind to it!
This is manly sorrow; these tears, I am very certain,
360 Never grew in my mother's milk. My estate
Is sunk below the degree of fear. Where were
These penitent fountains while she was living?
Oh, they were frozen up! Here is a sight
As direful to my soul as is the sword
365 Unto a wretch hath slain his father. Come, I'll bear thee
Hence, and execute thy last will; that's deliver
Thy body to the reverend dispose
Of some good women: that the cruel tyrant
Shall not deny me. Then I'll post to Milan,
370 Where somewhat I will speedily enact
Worth my dejection.   (*Exit [with the body]*)

339 stirs This incident parallels that of Desdemona's death
in Shakespeare's *Othello* 356 perspective telescope 367 dispose disposition

Act V

Scene I

(*Enter* Antonio *and* Delio)

Antonio.   What think you of my hope of reconcile-
  ment
To the Arragonian brethren?
    Delio.   I misdoubt it;
For though they have sent their letters of safe-conduct
For your repair to Milan, they appear
But nets to entrap you. The Marquis of Pescara,   5
Under whom you hold certain land in cheat,
Much 'gainst his noble nature hath been moved
To seize those lands, and some of his dependants
Are at this instant making it their suit
To be invested in your revenues.   10
I cannot think they mean well to your life
That do deprive you of your means of life,
Your living.
    Antonio.   You are still an heretic
To any safety I can shape myself.
    Delio.   Here comes the marquis. I will make myself 15
Petitioner for some part of your land,
To know whither it is flying.
    Antonio.   I pray do.
                                    (*Withdraws*)

(*Enter* Pescara)

Delio. Sir, I have a suit to you.
Pescara.   To me?

6 **in cheat** in the absence of lawful heirs; here used inaccu-
rately 10 **To be . . . revenues** to take over your income

81

DELIO.   An easy one.
20 There is the citadel of Saint Bennet,
With some demesnes, of late in the possession
Of Antonio Bologna, please you bestow them on me.
     PESCARA.   You are my friend, but this is such a suit,
Nor fit for me to give, nor you to take.
     DELIO.   No, sir?
25   PESCARA.   I will give you ample reason for 't
Soon in private. Here's the Cardinal's mistress.

(*Enter* JULIA)

     JULIA.   My lord, I am grown your poor petitioner,
And should be an ill beggar, had I not
A great man's letter here, the Cardinal's,
To court you in my favor.   (*Gives a letter*)
30   PESCARA.   He entreats for you
The citadel of Saint Bennet, that belonged
To the banished Bologna.
     JULIA.   Yes.
     PESCARA.   I could not
Have thought of a friend I could rather pleasure with it;
'Tis yours.
     JULIA.   Sir, I thank you; and he shall know
35 How doubly I am engaged both in your gift,
And speediness of giving, which makes your grant
The greater.   (*Exit*)
     ANTONIO.   (*aside*)   How they fortify themselves
With my ruin!
     DELIO.   Sir, I am little bound to you.
     PESCARA.   Why?
     DELIO.   Because you denied this suit to me, and
     gave 't
To such a creature.
40   PESCARA.   Do you know what it was?
It was Antonio's land, not forfeited
By course of law, but ravished from his throat
By the Cardinal's entreaty. It were not fit
I should bestow so main a piece of wrong
45 Upon my friend; 'tis a gratification
Only due to a strumpet, for it is injustice.

20 **Saint Bennet** St. Benedict, founder of the monastic order

Shall I sprinkle the pure blood of innocents
To make those followers I call my friends
Look ruddier upon me? I am glad
This land, ta'en from the owner by such wrong,   **50**
Returns again unto so foul an use
As salary for his lust. Learn, good Delio,
To ask noble things of me, and you shall find
I'll be a noble giver.
   DELIO.   You instruct me well.
   ANTONIO. (*aside*) Why, here's a man who would
     fright impudence   **55**
From sauciest beggars.
   PESCARA.   Prince Ferdinand's come to Milan,
Sick, as they give out, of an apoplexy,
But some say 'tis a frenzy. I am going
To visit him.   (*Exit*)
   ANTONIO. 'Tis a noble old fellow.
   DELIO.   What course do you mean to take, Antonio? **60**
   ANTONIO.   This night I mean to venture all my for-
     tune,
Which is no more than a poor lingering life,
To the Cardinal's worst of malice. I have got
Private access to his chamber, and intend
To visit him about the mid of night,   **65**
As once his brother did our noble duchess.
It may be that the sudden apprehension
Of danger—for I'll go in mine own shape—
When he shall see it fraught with love and duty,
May draw the poison out of him, and work   **70**
A friendly reconcilement. If it fail,
Yet it shall rid me of this infamous calling,
For better fall once than be ever falling.
   DELIO.   I'll second you in all danger, and, howe'er,
My life keeps rank with yours.
   ANTONIO.   You are still my loved **75**
And best friend.   (*Exeunt*)

84 JOHN WEBSTER [*Act V*]

Scene II

(*Enter* Pescara *and* Doctor)

PESCARA   Now, doctor, may I visit your patient?

DOCTOR.   If't please your lordship: but he's instantly
To take the air here in the gallery
By my direction.

PESCARA.   Pray thee, what's his disease?

5   DOCTOR.   A very pestilent disease, my lord,
They call lycanthropia.

PESCARA.   What's that?
I need a dictionary to 't.

DOCTOR.   I'll tell you.
In those that are possessed with 't there o'erflows
Such melancholy humor they imagine
10 Themselves to be transformèd into wolves;
Steal forth to churchyards in the dead of night,
And dig dead bodies up: as two nights since
One met the duke 'bout midnight in a lane
Behind Saint Mark's Church, with the leg of a man
15 Upon his shoulder; and he howled fearfully;
Said he was a wolf, only the difference
Was, a wolf's skin was hairy on the outside,
His on the inside; bade them take their swords,
Rip up his flesh, and try. Straight I was sent for,
20 And, having ministered to him, found his grace
Very well recovered.

PESCARA.   I am glad on 't.

DOCTOR.   Yet not without some fear
Of a relapse. If he grow to his fit again,
I'll go a nearer way to work with him
25 Than ever Paracelsus dreamed of: if
They'll give me leave, I'll buffet his madness
Out of him. Stand aside; he comes.

6 lycanthropia a form of insanity in which the patient believes that he is a wolf   9 melancholy humor one of the four fluids that, according to mediaeval physiology, determined the individual temperament   25 Paracelsus the famous German physician, half-quack, half-scientist, who died in 1541; here an anachronism

(*Enter* FERDINAND, MALATESTE, CARDINAL, and
BOSOLA)

FERDINAND.   Leave me.

MALATESTE.   Why doth your lordship love this solitariness?

FERDINAND.   Eagles commonly fly alone: they are **30**
crows, daws, and starlings that flock together. Look,
what's that follows me?

MALATESTE.   Nothing, my lord.

FERDINAND.   Yes.

MALATESTE.   'Tis your shadow.   **35**

FERDINAND.   Stay it; let it not haunt me.

MALATESTE.   Impossible, if you move, and the sun
shine.

FERDINAND.   I will throttle it.
                    (*Throws himself on the ground*)

MALATESTE.   O, my lord, you are angry with nothing. **40**

FERDINAND.   You are a fool: how is 't possible I
should catch my shadow, unless I fall upon 't? When
I go to hell, I mean to carry a bribe, for, look you, good
gifts evermore make way for the worst persons.

PESCARA.   Rise, good my lord.   **45**

FERDINAND.   I am studying the art of patience.

PESCARA.   'Tis a noble virtue.

FERDINAND.   To drive six snails before me from this
town to Moscow; neither use goad nor whip to them, but
let them take their own time—the patient'st man i' th' **50**
world match me for an experiment—and I'll crawl after
like a sheep-biter.

CARDINAL.   Force him up.   (*They raise him*)

FERDINAND.   Use me well, you were best. What I
have done, I have done: I'll confess nothing.   **55**

DOCTOR.   Now let me come to him. Are you mad,
my lord? Are you out of your princely wits?

FERDINAND.   What's he?

PESCARA.   Your doctor.

FERDINAND.   Let me have his beard sawed off, and **60**
his eyebrows filed more civil.

DOCTOR.   I must do mad tricks with him, for that's

52 **sheep-biter** a sneak-thief

the only way on 't. I have brought your grace a salamander's skin to keep you from sunburning.

65 FERDINAND.   I have cruel sore eyes.

DOCTOR.   The white of a cockatrix's egg is present
remedy.

FERDINAND.   Let it be a new laid one, you were best.
Hide me from him: physicians are like kings—they
70 brook no contradiction.

DOCTOR.   Now he begins to fear me: now let me
alone with him.

CARDINAL.   How now? Put off your gown?

DOCTOR.   Let me have some forty urinals filled with
75 rosewater: he and I'll go pelt one another with them.
Now he begins to fear me. Can you fetch a frisk, sir? Let
him go, let him go, upon my peril: I find by his eye he
stands in awe of me; I'll make him as tame as a dormouse.

80 FERDINAND.   Can you fetch your frisks, sir? I will
stamp him into a cullis, flay off his skin, to cover one
of the anatomies this rogue hath set i' th' cold yonder in
Barber-Chirurgeons'-Hall. Hence, hence! You are all of
you like beasts for sacrifice: there's nothing left of you
85 but tongue and belly, flattery and lechery.   (Exit)

PESCARA.   Doctor, he did not fear you throughly.

DOCTOR.   True;
I was somewhat too forward.

BOSOLA.   Mercy upon me,
What a fatal judgment hath fall'n upon this Ferdinand!

PESCARA.   Knows your grace what accident hath
          brought
90 Unto the prince this strange distraction?

CARDINAL.   (aside) I must feign somewhat. Thus
          they say it grew.
You have heard it rumored, for these many years
None of our family dies but there is seen
The shape of an old woman, which is given
95 By tradition to us to have been murdered
By her nephews for her riches. Such a figure
One night, as the prince sat up late at 's book,

66 present immediate 76 fetch a frisk cut a caper 82 anatomies skeletons 83 Chirurgeons Surgeons

Appeared to him; when, crying out for help,
The gentlemen of's chamber found His Grace
All on a cold sweat, altered much in face   100
And language, since which apparition,
He hath grown worse and worse, and I much fear
He cannot live.
   BOSOLA.   Sir, I would speak with you.
   PESCARA.   We'll leave Your Grace,
Wishing to the sick prince, our noble lord,   105
All health of mind and body.
   CARDINAL.   You are most welcome.
      (*Exeunt* PESCARA, MALATESTE, *and* DOCTOR)
Are you come? So. (*aside*) This fellow must not know
By any means I had intelligence
In our duchess' death; for, though I counselled it,
The full of all th' engagement seemed to grow   110
From Ferdinand. Now, sir, how fares our sister?
I do not think but sorrow makes her look
Like to an oft-dyed garment: she shall now
Taste comfort from me. Why do you look so wildly?
Oh, the fortune of your master here the prince   115
Dejects you, but be you of happy comfort:
If you'll do one thing for me I'll entreat,
Though he had a cold tombstone o'er his bones,
I'd make you what you would be.
   BOSOLA.   Anything;
Give it me in a breath, and let me fly to 't: 120
They that think long small expedition win,
For musing much o' th' end cannot begin.

         (*Enter* JULIA)

   JULIA.   Sir, will you come in to supper?
   CARDINAL.   I am busy;
Leave me.
   JULIA.   (*aside*) What an excellent shape hath that
    fellow!   (*Exit*) 125
   CARDINAL.   'Tis thus. Antonio lurks here in Milan:
Inquire him out, and kill him. While he lives,
Our sister cannot marry, and I have thought

121-122 They . . . begin idea taken from Sidney's *Arcadia*

Of an excellent match for her. Do this, and style me
130 Thy advancement.

BOSOLA.   But by what means shall I find him out?

CARDINAL.   There is a gentleman called Delio
Here in the camp, that hath been long approved
His loyal friend. Set eye upon that fellow;
135 Follow him to mass; maybe Antonio,
Although he do account religion
But a school-name, for fashion of the world
May accompany him; or else go inquire out
Delio's confessor, and see if you can bribe
140 Him to reveal it. There are a thousand ways
A man might find to trace him; as to know
What fellows haunt the Jews for taking up
Great sums of money, for sure he 's in want;
Or else to go to th' picture-makers, and learn
145 Who bought her picture lately. Some of these
Happily may take.

BOSOLA.   Well, I'll not freeze i' th' business:
I would see that wretched thing, Antonio,
Above all sights i' th' world.

CARDINAL.   Do, and be happy. (*Exit*)

BOSOLA.   This fellow doth breed basilisks in 's eyes,
150 He's nothing else but murder; yet he seems
Not to have notice of the duchess' death.
'Tis his cunning: I must follow his example;
There cannot be a surer way to trace
Than that of an old fox.

     (*Re-enter* JULIA, *with a pistol*)

155 JULIA.   So, sir, you are well met.

BOSOLA.   How now?

JULIA.   Nay, the doors are fast enough.
Now, sir,
I will make you confess your treachery.

BOSOLA.   Treachery?

JULIA.   Yes,
160 Confess to me which of my women 'twas
You hired to put love-powder into my drink?

137 But a school-name merely a philosophical term 153
trace follow

BOSOLA.   Love-powder?

JULIA.   Yes, when I was at Malfi.
Why should I fall in love with such a face else?
I have already suffered for thee so much pain,
The only remedy to do me good   **165**
Is to kill my longing.

BOSOLA.   Sure, your pistol holds
Nothing but perfumes or kissing-comfits.
Excellent lady! You have a pretty way on 't
To discover your longing. Come, come, I'll disarm you,
And arm you thus: yet this is wondrous strange.   **170**

   JULIA.   Compare thy form and my eyes together,
      you'll find
My love no such great miracle. Now you'll say
I am wanton: this nice modesty in ladies
Is but a troublesome familiar that haunts them.

   BOSOLA.   Know you me, I am a blunt soldier.

JULIA.   The better: **175**
Sure, there wants fire where there are no lively sparks
Of roughness.

   BOSOLA.   And I want compliment.

JULIA.   Why, ignorance
In courtship cannot make you do amiss,
If you have a heart to do well.

   BOSOLA.   You are very fair.   **180**

   JULIA.   Nay, if you lay beauty to my charge,
I must plead unguilty.

   BOSOLA.   Your bright eyes carry
A quiver of darts in them sharper than sunbeams.

   JULIA.   You will mar me with commendation,
Put yourself to the charge of courting me,   **185**
Whereas now I woo you.

   BOSOLA.   (*aside*) I have it, I will work upon this
      creature.
Let us grow most amorously familiar.
If the great Cardinal now should see me thus,
Would he not count me a villain?

   JULIA.   No; he might   **190**
Count me a wanton, not lay a scruple

167 kissing-comfits sweets for the breath 170 arm embrace
174 familiar spirit 177 want am lacking in

Of offence on you; for if I see and steal
A diamond, the fault is not i' th' stone,
But in me the thief that purloins it. I am sudden
195 With you: we that are great women of pleasure
Use to cut off these uncertain wishes
And unquiet longings, and in an instant join
The sweet delight and the pretty excuse together.
Had you been i' th' street, under my chamber-window,
Even there I should have courted you.
200   BOSOLA.   Oh, you are
An excellent lady!
        JULIA.   Bid me do somewhat for you
Presently to express I love you.
        BOSOLA.   I will;
And if you love me, fail not to effect it.
The Cardinal is grown wondrous melancholy;
205 Demand the cause, let him not put you off
With feigned excuse; discover the main ground on 't.
        JULIA. Why would you know this?
        BOSOLA.   I have depended on him,
And I hear that he is fallen in some disgrace
With the emperor: if he be, like the mice
210 That forsake falling houses, I would shift
To other dependence.
        JULIA.   You shall not need
Follow the wars: I'll be your maintenance.
        BOSOLA. And I your loyal servant: but I cannot
Leave my calling.
        JULIA.   Not leave an ungrateful
215 General for the love of a sweet lady?
You are like some cannot sleep in feather-beds,
But must have blocks for their pillows.
        BOSOLA.   Will you do this?
        JULIA. Cunningly.
        BOSOLA. Tomorrow I'll expect th' intelligence.
220   JULIA. Tomorrow? Get you into my cabinet;
You shall have it with you. Do not delay me,
No more than I do you: I am like one
That is condemned; I have my pardon promised,

207 depended on him been one of his followers

But I would see it sealed. Go, get you in:
You shall see me wind my tongue about his heart   225
Like a skein of silk.   (*Exit* BOSOLA)

                    (*Re-enter* CARDINAL)

CARDINAL.   Where are you?

                    (*Enter* SERVANTS)

SERVANTS.   Here.
CARDINAL.   Let none, upon your lives, have con-
    ference
With the Prince Ferdinand, unless I know it.
(*aside*) In this distraction he may reveal
The murder.   (*Exeunt* SERVANTS)
                    Yond's my lingering consumption: 230
I am weary of her, and by any means
Would be quit of.
    JULIA.   How now, my lord? What ails you?
    CARDINAL.   Nothing.
    JULIA.   Oh, you are much altered: come, I must be
Your secretary, and remove this lead   235
From off your bosom. What's the matter?
    CARDINAL.   I may not
Tell you.
    JULIA.   Are you so far in love with sorrow
You cannot part with part of it? Or think you
I cannot love your grace when you are sad
As well as merry? Or do you suspect   240
I, that have been a secret to your heart
These many winters, cannot be the same
Unto your tongue?
    CARDINAL.   Satisfy thy longing—
The only way to make thee keep my counsel
Is not to tell thee.
    JULIA.   Tell your echo this,   245
Or flatterers, that like echoes still report
What they hear though most imperfect, and not me;
For if that you be true unto yourself,
I'll know.
    CARDINAL.   Will you rack me?

235 **secretary** confidante   249 **rack me** put me to the rack

JULIA.   No, judgment shall
250 Draw it from you: it is an equal fault,
To tell one's secrets unto all or none.
    CARDINAL.   The first argues folly.
    JULIA.   But the last, tyranny.
    CARDINAL.   Very well. Why, imagine I have com-
        mitted
Some secret deed which I desire the world
May never hear of.
255   JULIA.   Therefore may not I know it?
You have concealed for me as great a sin
As adultery. Sir, never was occasion
For perfect trial of my constancy
Till now: sir, I beseech you——
    CARDINAL.   You'll repent it.
260   JULIA. Never.
    CARDINAL.   It hurries thee to ruin: I'll not tell thee.
Be well advised, and think what danger 'tis
To receive a prince's secrets: they that do,
Had need have their breasts hooped with adamant
265 To contain them. I pray thee, yet be satisfied;
Examine thine own frailty; 'tis more easy
To tie knots than unloose them: 'tis a secret
That, like a lingering poison, may chance lie
Spread in thy veins, and kill thee seven year hence.
    JULIA.   Now you dally with me.
270   CARDINAL.   No more; thou shalt know it.
By my appointment the great Duchess of Malfi
And two of her young children, four nights since,
Were strangled.
    JULIA.   O Heaven! Sir, what have you done!
    CARDINAL.   How now? How settles this? Think you
        your bosom
275 Will be a grave dark and obscure enough
For such a secret?
    JULIA.   You have undone yourself, sir.
    CARDINAL.   Why?
    JULIA.   It lies not in me to conceal it.
    CARDINAL.   No?
Come, I will swear you to 't upon this book.
    JULIA.   Most religiously.

CARDINAL.   Kiss it. (*She kisses the book*)
                                  Now you shall
Never utter it; thy curiosity   280
Hath undone thee: thou'rt poisoned with that book.
Because I knew thou couldst not keep my counsel,
I have bound thee to 't by death.

                    (*Re-enter* BOSOLA)

BOSOLA.   For pity sake,
Hold!
    CARDINAL.   Ha! Bosola?
    JULIA.   I forgive you
This equal piece of justice you have done;   285
For I betrayed your counsel to that fellow:
He overheard it; that was the cause I said
It lay not in me to conceal it.
    BOSOLA.   O foolish woman,
Couldst not thou have poisoned him?
    JULIA.   'Tis weakness,
Too much to think what should have been done. I go   290
I know not whither.   (*Dies*)
    CARDINAL.   Wherefore com'st thou hither?
    BOSOLA.   That I might find a great man like yourself,
Not out of his wits as the Lord Ferdinand,
To remember my service.
    CARDINAL.   I'll have thee hewed in pieces.
    BOSOLA.   Make not yourself such a promise of that
        life   295
Which is not yours to dispose of.
    CARDINAL.   Who placed thee here?
    BOSOLA.   Her lust, as she intended.
    CARDINAL.   Very well.
Now you know me for your fellow-murderer.
    BOSOLA.   And wherefore should you lay fair marble
        colors
Upon your rotten purposes to me?   300
Unless you imitate some that do plot great treasons,
And when they have done, go hide themselves i' th'
        graves

299 **fair marble colors** paint applied so as to make wood
resemble marble

Of those were actors in 't?

CARDINAL.   No more; there is
A fortune attends thee.

BOSOLA.   Shall I go sue
305 To Fortune any longer? 'Tis the fool's
Pilgrimage.

    CARDINAL. I have honors in store for thee.

    BOSOLA. There are a many ways that conduct to
        seeming
Honor, and some of them very dirty ones.

    CARDINAL.   Throw
To the devil thy melancholy. The fire burns well;
310 What need we keep a stirring of 't, and make
A greater smother? Thou wilt kill Antonio?

    BOSOLA. Yes.

    CARDINAL. Take up that body.

    BOSOLA.   I think I shall
Shortly grow the common beare[r] for churchyards.

    CARDINAL. I will allow thee some dozen of attend-
        ants
315 To aid thee in the murder.

    BOSOLA. Oh, by no means. Physicians that apply
horse-leeches to any rank swelling use to cut off their
tails, that the blood may run through them the faster: let
me have no train when I go to shed blood, lest it make
320 me have a greater when I ride to the gallows.

    CARDINAL. Come to me after midnight, to help to
        remove
That body to her own lodging: I'll give out
She died o' th' plague; 'twill breed the less inquiry
After her death.

    BOSOLA.   Where's Castruccio her husband?

325   CARDINAL. He's rode to Naples, to take possession
Of Antonio's citadel.

    BOSOLA.   Believe me, you have done
A very happy turn.

    CARDINAL.   Fail not to come.
There is the master-key of our lodgings, and by that
You may conceive what trust I plant in you.

    BOSOLA. You shall find me ready. (*Exit* [CARDINAL])
330   O poor Antonio,

Though nothing be so needful to thy estate
As pity, yet I find nothing so dangerous;
I must look to my footing:
In such slippery ice-pavements men had need
To be frost-nailed well; they may break their necks else; 335
The precedent's here afore me. How this man
Bears up in blood! Seems fearless! Why, 'tis well:
Security some men call the suburbs of hell,
Only a dead wall between. Well, good Antonio,
I'll seek thee out, and all my care shall be 340
To put thee into safety from the reach
Of these most cruel biters that have got
Some of thy blood already. It may be,
I'll join with thee in a most just revenge:
The weakest arm is strong enough that strikes 345
With the sword of justice. Still methinks the duchess
Haunts me. There, there, 'tis nothing but my melancholy.
O Penitence, let me truly taste thy cup,
That throws men down only to raise them up! (*Exit*)

SCENE III

([*Enter*] ANTONIO *and* DELIO. *Echo from the
Duchess' grave*)

DELIO.   Yond's the Cardinal's window. This fortifica-
tion
Grew from the ruins of an ancient abbey;
And to yond side o' th' river lies a wall,
Piece of a cloister, which in my opinion
Gives the best echo that you ever heard, 5
So hollow and so dismal, and withal
So plain in the distinction of our words,
That many have supposed it is a spirit
That answers.
ANTONIO.   I do love these ancient ruins.
We never tread upon them but we set 10
Our foot upon some reverend history:
And, questionless, here in this open court,
Which now lies naked to the injuries

337 **bears up in blood** keeps up his courage 9-11 **I do love
. . . history** idea borrowed from Montaigne's *Essays*

Of stormy weather, some men lie interred
15 Loved the church so well, and gave so largely to 't,
They thought it should have canopied their bones
Till doomsday; but all things have their end:
Churches and cities, which have diseases
Like to men, must have like death that we have.

20   ECHO.   "Like death that we have."
    DELIO.   Now the echo hath caught you.
    ANTONIO.   It groaned, methought, and gave
A very deadly accent.
    ECHO.   "Deadly accent."
    DELIO.   I told you 'twas a pretty one: you may
    make it
25 A huntsman, or a falconer, a musician,
Or a thing of sorrow.
    ECHO.   "A thing of sorrow."
    ANTONIO.   Aye, sure, that suits it best.
    ECHO.   "That suits it best."
    ANTONIO.   'Tis very like my wife's voice.
    ECHO.   "Aye, wife's voice."
    DELIO.   Come, let's walk further from 't. I would
    not have you
Go to th' Cardinal's to-night: do not.
30   ECHO.   "Do not."
    DELIO.   Wisdom doth not more moderate wasting
    sorrow
Than time: take time for 't; be mindful of thy safety.
    ECHO.   "Be mindful of thy safety."
    ANTONIO.   Necessity compels me:
Make scrutiny throughout the passes of
35 Your own life, you'll find it impossible
To fly your fate.
    ECHO.   "Oh, fly your fate."
    DELIO.   Hark!
The dead stones seem to have pity on you, and give you
Good counsel.
    ANTONIO.   Echo, I will not talk with thee,

20 **Like death that we have** This echo-scene is a conven-
tion of classical drama widely imitated by Renaissance play-
wrights. Webster probably borrowed it from one of his favorite books, Sidney's *Arcadia*

For thou art a dead thing.
    ECHO.   "Thou art a dead thing."
    ANTONIO.   My duchess is asleep now,   40
And her little ones, I hope sweetly: O Heaven,
Shall I never see her more?
    ECHO.   "Never see her more."
    ANTONIO.   I marked not one repetition of the echo
But that, and on the sudden a clear light
Presented me a face folded in sorrow.   45
    DELIO.   Your fancy merely.
    ANTONIO.   Come, I'll be out of this ague,
For to live thus is not indeed to live;
It is a mockery and abuse of life.
I will not henceforth save myself by halves;
Lose all, or nothing.
    DELIO.   Your own virtue save you!   50
I'll fetch your eldest son, and second you:
It may be that the sight of his own blood
Spread in so sweet a figure may beget
The more compassion. However, fare you well.
Though in our miseries Fortune have a part,   55
Yet in our noble sufferings she hath none:
Contempt of pain, that we may call our own.
                                (*Exe*[*unt*])

SCENE IV

(*Enter* CARDINAL, PESCARA, MALATESTE, RODERIGO,
and GRISOLAN)

    CARDINAL.   You shall not watch to-night by the sick
      prince;
His Grace is very well recovered.
    MALATESTE.   Good my lord, suffer us.
    CARDINAL.   Oh, by no means;
The noise and change of object in his eye
Doth more distract him. I pray, all to bed;   5
And though you hear him in his violent fit,
Do not rise, I entreat you.
    PESCARA.   So, sir; we shall not.

43 **marked** heeded   3 **suffer** permit

CARDINAL.   Nay, I must have you promise upon
   your honors,
For I was enjoined to 't by himself; and he seemed
To urge it sensibly.
10   PESCARA.   Let our honors bind
This trifle.
        CARDINAL.   Nor any of your followers.
        MALATESTE.   Neither.
        CARDINAL.   It may be, to make trial of your promise,
When he's asleep, myself will rise and feign
Some of his mad tricks, and cry out for help,
And feign myself in danger.
15   MALATESTE.   If your throat were cutting,
I'd not come at you, now I have protested against it.
        CARDINAL.   Why, I thank you.
        GRISOLAN.   'Twas a foul storm tonight.
        RODERIGO.   The Lord Ferdinand's chamber shook
   like an osier.
        MALATESTE.   'Twas nothing but pure kindness in the
   devil,
20 To rock his own child.
                    (*Exeunt [all except the* CARDINAL])
        CARDINAL.   The reason why I would not suffer these
About my brother, is, because at midnight
I may with better privacy convey
Julia's body to her own lodging. Oh, my conscience!
25 I would pray now, but the devil takes away my heart
For having any confidence in prayer.
About this hour I appointed Bosola
To fetch the body: when he hath served my turn,
He dies.   (*Exit*)
                (*Enter* BOSOLA)

        BOSOLA.   Ha! 'Twas the Cardinal's voice; I heard
30   him name
Bosola and my death. Listen! I hear
One's footing.
                (*Enter* FERDINAND)

        FERDINAND.   Strangling is a very quiet death.

25-26 **I would pray . . . prayer** a reminiscence of *Hamlet*.
III. iii.

BOSOLA. (*aside*) Nay, then, I see I must stand upon
my guard.

FERDINAND. What say to that? Whisper softly; do 35
you agree to 't? So; it must be done i' th' dark: the
Cardinal would not for a thousand pounds the doctor
should see it.

BOSOLA. My death is plotted; here 's the conse-
quence of murder.

We value not desert nor Christian breath,   40
When we know black deeds must be cured with death.

(*Enter* ANTONIO *and* SERVANT)

SERVANT. Here stay, sir, and be confident, I pray:
I'll fetch you a dark lantern.   (*Exit*)

ANTONIO.   Could I take him
At his prayers, there were hope of pardon.

BOSOLA.   Fall right, my sword! (*Stabs him*)
I'll not give thee so much leisure as to pray.   45

ANTONIO. Oh, I am gone! Thou hast ended a long
suit

In a minute.

BOSOLA. What art thou?

ANTONIO.   A most wretched thing,
That only have thy benefit in death,
To appear myself.

(*Re-enter* SERVANT *with a lantern*)

SERVANT.   Where are you, sir?   50

ANTONIO. Very near my home. Bosola?

SERVANT.   Oh, misfortune!

BOSOLA. Smother thy pity; thou art dead else. Antonio?

The man I would have saved 'bove mine own life!
We are merely the stars' tennis-balls, struck and bandied
Which way please them. O good Antonio,   55
I'll whisper one thing in thy dying ear
Shall make thy heart break quickly! Thy fair duchess
And two sweet children——

ANTONIO.   Their very names
Kindle a little life in me.

BOSOLA.   Are murdered.

60   ANTONIO. Some men have wished to die
At the hearing of sad tidings; I am glad
That I shall do 't in sadness: I would not now
Wish my wounds balmed nor healed, for I have no use
To put my life to. In all our quest of greatness,
65 Like wanton boys, whose pastime is their care,
We follow after bubbles blown in th' air.
Pleasure of life, what is 't? Only the good
Hours of an ague; merely a preparative
To rest, to endure vexation. I do not ask
70 The process of my death; only commend me
To Delio.
      BOSOLA. Break, heart!
      ANTONIO.   And let my son
Fly the courts of princes.   (*Dies*)
      BOSOLA.   Thou seem'st
To have loved Antonio?
      SERVANT.   I brought him hither,
To have reconciled him to the Cardinal.
75 BOSOLA. I do not ask thee that.
Take him up, if thou tender thine own life,
And bear him where the lady Julia
Was wont to lodge. Oh, my fate moves swift;
I have this Cardinal in the forge already;
80 Now I'll bring him to th' hammer. O direful misprison!
I will not imitate things glorious,
No more than base; I'll be mine own example.
On, on, and look thou represent, for silence,
The thing thou bear'st.   (*Exeunt*)

SCENE V

([*Enter*] CARDINAL, *with a book*)

CARDINAL. I am puzzled in a question about hell:
He says, in hell there 's one material fire,
And yet it shall not burn all men alike.
Lay him by. How tedious is a guilty conscience!
5 When I look into the fish-ponds in my garden,

62 in sadness really 80 misprison error 5-7 When I look
. . . me idea and phrasing from the translation of Lavater's
Of Ghosts and Spirits Walking by Night

Methinks I see a thing armed with a rake,
That seems to strike at me.

(*Enter* BOSOLA, *and Servant bearing* ANTONIO's *body*)

                   Now, art thou come?
Thou look'st ghastly:
There sits in thy face some great determination
Mixed with some fear.
    BOSOLA.   Thus it lightens into action: **10**
I am come to kill thee.
    CARDINAL.   Ha! Help! Our guard!
    BOSOLA.   Thou art deceived; they are out of thy
      howling.
    CARDINAL.   Hold; and I will faithfully divide
Revenues with thee.
    BOSOLA.   Thy prayers and proffers
Are both unseasonable.
    CARDINAL.   Raise the watch!   **15**
We are betrayed!
    BOSOLA.   I have confined your flight:
I'll suffer your retreat to Julia's chamber,
But no further.
    CARDINAL.   Help! We are betrayed!

(*Enter, above,* PESCARA, MALATESTE, RODERIGO, *and*
               GRISOLAN)

    MALATESTE.   Listen.
    CARDINAL.   My dukedom for rescue!
    RODERIGO.   Fie upon **20**
His counterfeiting!
    MALATESTE.   Why, 'tis not the Cardinal.
    RODERIGO.   Yes, yes, 'tis he, but I'll see him hanged
Ere I'll go down to him.
    CARDINAL.   Here's a plot upon me;
I am assaulted! I am lost, unless some rescue.
    GRISOLAN.   He doth this pretty well, but it will not
      serve   **25**
To laugh me out of mine honor.
    CARDINAL.   The sword's at my throat!
    RODERIGO.   You would not bawl so loud then.
    MALATESTE.   Come, come,

Let 's go to bed. He told us thus much aforehand.

PESCARA.   He wished you should not come at him;
but, believe 't,

30 The accent of the voice sounds not in jest:
I'll down to him, howsoever, and with engines
Force ope the doors.   (*Exit above*)

RODERIGO.   Let's follow him aloof,
And note how the Cardinal will laugh at him.

(*Exeunt, above,* MALATESTE, RODERIGO,
and GRISOLAN)

BOSOLA.   There's for first,   (*He kills the Servant*)

35 'Cause you shall not unbarricade the door
To let in rescue.

CARDINAL.   What cause hast thou to pursue my life?

BOSOLA.   Look there.

CARDINAL.   Antonio?

BOSOLA.   Slain by my hand unwittingly.
Pray, and be sudden: when thou killed'st thy sister,

40 Thou took'st from Justice her most equal balance,
And left her naught but her sword.

CARDINAL.   Oh, mercy!

BOSOLA.   Now, it seems thy greatness was only out-
ward;
For thou fall'st faster of thyself than calamity
Can drive thee. I'll not waste longer time; there!

(*Stabs him*)

CARDINAL.   Thou hast hurt me.

BOSOLA.   Again!

(*Stabs him again*)

45 CARDINAL.   Shall I die like a leveret,
Without any resistance? Help, help, help!
I am slain!

(*Enter* FERDINAND)

FERDINAND.   Th' alarum? Give me a fresh horse;
Rally the vaunt-guard, or the day is lost.
Yield, yield! I give you the honor of arms,

31 **engines** tools 35 **'Cause** So that 45 **leveret** rabbit 49
honor of arms fair terms of surrender

Shake my sword over you; will you yield?   **50**
    CARDINAL.   Help me; I am your brother!
    FERDINAND.   The devill!
My brother fight upon the adverse party?
       (*He wounds the* CARDINAL, *and, in the scuffle,*
               gives BOSOLA *his death-wound*)
There flies your ransom.
    CARDINAL.   O justice!
I suffer now for what hath former been: **55**
Sorrow is held the eldest child of sin.
    FERDINAND.   Now you 're brave fellows. Caesar's
fortune was harder than Pompey's; Caesar died in the
arms of prosperity, Pompey at the feet of disgrace.
You both died in the field. The pain 's nothing: pain **60**
many times is taken away with the apprehension of
greater, as the toothache with the sight of a barber that
comes to pull it out: there's philosophy for you.
    BOSOLA.   Now my revenge is perfect. Sink, thou
    main cause   (*He kills* FERDINAND)
Of my undoing! The last part of my life   **65**
Hath done me best service.
    FERDINAND.   Give me some wet hay; I am broken-
winded. I do account this world but a dog-kennel: I
will vault credit and affect high pleasures beyond death.
    BOSOLA.   He seems to come to himself, now he 's
    so near   **70**
The bottom.
    FERDINAND.   My sister, O my sister! There 's the
    cause on 't.
Whether we fall by ambition, blood, or lust,
Like diamonds we are cut with our own dust.   (*Dies*)
    CARDINAL.   Thou hast thy payment, too.   **75**
    BOSOLA.   Yes, I hold my weary soul in my teeth.
'Tis ready to part from me. I do glory
That thou, which stood'st like a huge pyramid
Begun upon a large and ample base,
Shalt end in a little point, a kind of nothing.   **80**

69 **vault credit** disregard probability **affect** aspire to

(*Enter, below,* PESCARA, MALATESTE, RODERIGO,
            and GRISOLAN)

PESCARA.   How now, my lord?
MALATESTE.   O sad disaster!
RODERIGO.   How
Comes this?
BOSOLA.   Revenge for the Duchess of Malfi murdered
By th' Arragonian brethren; for Antonio
85 Slain by [t]his hand; for lustful Julia
Poisoned by this man; and lastly for myself,
That was an actor in the main of all,
Much 'gainst mine own good nature, yet i' th' end
Neglected.
90   PESCARA.   How now, my lord?
        CARDINAL.   Look to my brother: he gave us these
            large wounds
As we were struggling here i' the rushes. And now,
I pray, let me be laid by and never thought of. (*Dies*)
        PESCARA.   How fatally, it seems, he did withstand
His own rescue!
95   MALATESTE.   Thou wretched thing of blood,
How came Antonio by his death?
        BOSOLA.   In a mist;
I know not how: such a mistake as I
Have often seen in a play. Oh, I am gone!
We are only like dead walls or vaulted graves,
100 That, ruined, yield no echo. Fare you well.
It may be pain, but no harm, to me to die
In so good a quarrel. Oh, this gloomy world!
In what a shadow, or deep pit of darkness,
Doth, womanish and fearful, mankind live!
105 Let worthy minds ne'er stagger in distrust
To suffer death or shame for what is just:
Mine is another voyage.   (*Dies*)
        PESCARA.   The noble Delio, as I came to the palace,
Told me of Antonio's being here, and showed me
110 A pretty gentleman, his son and heir.

92 **rushes** the usual Elizabethan covering for stone floors
103-104 **In what . . . live** idea and phrasing from Sidney's
Arcadia

(*Enter* DELIO *and* ANTONIO's *Son*)

MALATESTE.   O sir,
You come too late!
    DELIO.   I heard so, and was armed for 't
Ere I came. Let us make noble use
Of this great ruin; and join all our force
To establish this young hopeful gentleman   115
In 's mother's right. These wretched eminent things
Leave no more fame behind 'em, than should one
Fall in a frost, and leave his print in snow;
As soon as the sun shines, it ever melts,
Both form and matter. I have ever thought   120
Nature doth nothing so great for great men
As when she 's pleased to make them lords of truth:
Integrity of life is fame's best friend,
Which nobly, beyond death, shall crown the end.
                          (*Exeunt*)

BIBLIOGRAPHY

EDITIONS

Brown, John Russell, ed., *John Webster, The Duchess of Malfi*, "The Revels Plays" (Cambridge, Mass., 1964).

Lucas, Frank L., ed., *The Complete Works of John Webster* (London, 1927). 4 volumes.

Lucas, Frank L., ed., *The Duchess of Malfi* (Macmillan, 1959).

Rylands, George and Williams, Charles, ed., *The Duchess of Malfi* (London, 1945).

Sampson, Martin W., ed., *The White Devil* and *The Duchess of Malfi*, "The Belles-Lettres Series" (Boston and London, 1904).

Symonds, John A., ed., *Webster & Tourneur*, "The Mermaid Series" (New York, 1893).

Thorndike, Ashley H., ed., *Webster and Tourneur*, "Masterpieces of English Drama" (New York, etc., 1912).

Vaughan, Charles E., ed., *The Duchess of Malfi*, "Temple Dramatists Series" (London, 1896).

CRITICISM

Lamb, Charles, *Specimens of English Dramatic Poets* (London, 1808).

Hazlitt, William, *Lectures on the Dramatic Literature of the Age of Elizabeth* (London, 1820).

Swinburne, Algernon C., "John Webster," *The Nineteenth Century*, June, 1886, pp. 861-881. A revision of this essay was printed in *The Age of Shakespeare* (New York and London, 1908).

Archer, William, "Webster, Lamb, and Swinburne," *New Review*, VIII (1893), 96 ff. Archer repeated his attack on the play in "The Duchess of Malfi," *The Nineteenth Century*, January, 1920, pp. 126-132 and in *The Old Drama and the New* (Boston, 1923).

Stoll, Elmer E., *John Webster* (Cambridge, Mass., 1905).

Brooke, Rupert, *John Webster and the Elizabethan Drama* (London, 1917).

Edwards, M. C., "John Webster," in *Determinations*, edited by Frank R. Leavis (London, 1934).

Bradbrook, M. C., *Themes and Conventions of Elizabethan Tragedy* (Cambridge, 1935).

Ellis-Fermor, Una, *The Jacobean Drama* (London, 1936).

Anderson, Marcia L., "Webster's Debt to Guazzo," *Studies in Philology*, XXXVI (1939), 192-205.

Bowers, Fredson T., *Elizabethan Revenge Tragedy* (Princeton, 1940).

Leech, Clifford, *John Webster, a critical study*, "Hogarth Lectures on Literature, 16," London, 1951.

Bogard, Travis, *The Tragic Satire of John Webster* (Berkeley, 1955).

Price, Hereward T., "The Function of Imagery in Webster," *Publications of the Modern Language Association*, LXX (1955), 717-39.

Davies, Cecil W., "The Structure of *The Duchess of Malfi*," *English*, XII (1958), 89-93.

Ekeblad, Inga-Stina, "The 'Impure Art' of John Webster," *Review of English Studies*, n. s., IX (1958), 253-67.

Emslie, McD., "Motives in Malfi," *Essays in Criticism*, IX (1959), 391-405.

Dent, Robert W., *John Webster's Borrowing* (Berkeley, 1960).

Mulryne, J. R., "*The White Devil* and *The Duchess of Malfi*," *Stratford-upon-Avon Studies, I: Jacobean Theatre*, 200-225 (London, 1960).

Ornstein, Robert, *The Moral Vision of Jacobean Tragedy* (Madison, 1960).

Boklund, Gunnar, *The Duchess of Malfi: Sources, Themes, Characters* (Cambridge, Mass., 1962).

Ribner, Irving, *Jacobean Tragedy* (London, 1962).

Leech, Clifford, *The Duchess of Malfi*, "Studies in English Literature, 8" (London, 1963).